I CAUGHT FLIES FOR
Howard Hughes

I CAUGHT FLIES FOR

Howard Hughes

RON KISTLER

ꠗꠗP
A PLAYBOY PRESS BOOK

To Virgie

FIRST EDITION.
Playboy and Rabbit Head design are trademarks of Playboy, 919 North Michi-
gan Avenue, Chicago, Illinois 60611 (U.S.A.), Reg. U.S. Pat. Off., marca
registrada, marque déposée.

Library of Congress Cataloging in Publication Data

Kistler, Ron.
    I caught flies for Howard Hughes.
        1. Hughes, Howard Robard, 1905–   2. Kistler, Ron. I. Title.
CT275.H6678K57   670'.92'4 [B]   75-45271
ISBN 0-87223-447-9

Acknowledgments

There may be a few books that appear each year for which the author can claim sole credit; this is not one of them. There are a number of people whose help was vital to me in getting this book into your hands.

My wife, Virgie, supplied an abundance of faith and love from the day that we met. She struck the match that started this project, nurtured the sparks with confidence and compassion, and fanned the fire when my self-doubt and impatience could have let it die. I will spend the rest of my life trying to repay her for all that she has meant —and still means—to me.

My children, their spouses, and their children deserve more than thanks. The years that are described in this book were responsible for depriving my kids of an in-home father. I'm happy that that absence did not leave any lasting scars on my kids, and that they have been loving, proud, and unselfish.

My mother, Lucy Kistler, is responsible for my independent nature. She taught me to think for myself and stand up and fight for my beliefs, although I'm sure that she never dreamed that one day I'd be standing up to Howard Hughes.

Ed Kuhn of Playboy Press and G. Barry Golson of *Playboy* magazine were my twin entrees into the world of publishing. I'm deeply grateful that both men had the wisdom *and* the balls to tackle a project that had scared other editors. Ed Kuhn's successor at the Press, Paul Lapolla, and Michael Cohn on the administrative side, have been most helpful, and extremely patient as I learned about the mechanics of being an author.

My attorney, Declan J. O'Donnell, has had the awesome task of guiding this project through a tangled legal maze. He has been skillful and conscientious and has taken what would have been an oppressive burden from my shoulders.

Behind every book there is an agent. The late Peter Kemeny used what tragically turned out to be his last resources on behalf of this project. The team of Susan Gross and Debra Greenfield have since provided great quantities of what every writer needs—enthusiasm and support.

Words cannot begin to express my debt to Lawrence Dietz. His official function was to edit and polish the manuscript. What he wound up doing was to turn a mountain of unrelated, rough pages into a smooth, professional piece of work—and one that spoke in my voice. Larry did this with an extraordinary amount of dedication, talent, and a terrific sense of humor. He not only got into my head and my mind, but he has a large part of my heart.

Finally, I'd like to pay tribute to *Musta domestica*—the common house fly. Were it not for the sex habits and generous reproductive instincts of these insects I might not have been able to be as close to Howard Hughes as I was.

I CAUGHT FLIES FOR
Howard Hughes

Introduction

One hot day during the summer of 1958 I was standing in a darkened corner of the living room of Bungalow Four of the Beverly Hills Hotel, waiting for the right moment to make my move against a fly that was buzzing around the room.

The man who lived in the $175-a-day bungalow, my employer, paid three men to be on call, 24 hours a day, to walk from *their* $175-a-day bungalow at the hotel to his, whenever he phoned. One of them would stand by his door whenever it was opened or closed and wave a newspaper at the doorway to discourage any insect from flying into the bungalow.

But this little devil had gotten in. On hot sunny days flies made kamikaze dives to get into the darkness of Bungalow Four. It was dark because my employer kept the lights off and the drapes closed. It was also warm, since he kept the air conditioners off, preferring to sit nude in a white leather chair—nude, that is, save for a pink hotel napkin, which he kept on his crotch. Perhaps today's fly only wanted to get inside to see the movie I had been screening for my employer. My job was to run the projector, but I did a lot more for my salary.

Like going after flies. My employer watched me watching for the insect. While he was sitting there, he kept stacking and restacking Kleenex boxes on a table next to his chair. There was always plenty of Kleenex in the room, not only in those boxes but also used tissues on the floor, where he would throw them after wiping down every surface within his reach.

There was another piece of Kleenex, a clean sheet, resting on my right palm. I wasn't allowed to use a fly swatter, newspaper or magazine, sticky paper, or spray can when I went after a fly in Bungalow Four. It was hand-to-wing combat, and the Kleenex was there to ensure that the hand would never come into direct contact with the foe. I had to move very slowly. Any sudden action on my part would not only alert the fly but, worse, would raise a cloud of dust in the incredibly messy, littered room. Patience was the key to this hunt: my employer had patience, the fly had patience, and so I had to have patience.

I had learned from experience that the best time to swipe at the fly would be just before it took off, and when it was in a relatively dust-free location. Flies jump backward when they take off, so I knew how to aim my swipe.

Got it! My employer always insisted that he personally see the fallen enemy, so I had to go over to his chair, stand in front of him, extend my arm to a position eight inches from his nose, unfold the tissue, and let him inspect the kill. He rarely commented, but this time he said, "That's a nice fly, Ron." I didn't say anything in response to that compliment, because I was not supposed to speak in his presence. I was spending 8 to 16 hours a day in Bungalow Four, not talking, showing movies for my employer.

His name was Howard Hughes. It was the oddest period of my life.

*　*　*

During the past several years I've read a lot of material about the fabled Howard Hughes. It's been written by every breed of cat: those who have heard Hughes; those who have seen Hughes; those who *wish* they had seen or heard Hughes; and one thing by a writer who seemed to think he *was* Hughes.

None of what I've read has been half as interesting, or funny, as what happened during the time *I* spent with Howard Hughes, and so with each reading I've been pushed closer to the inevitable decision: It's *my* turn!

My qualifications for writing about Hughes are that I was employed by Hughes Productions for a three-year period, during which I was thrown into contact with Howard Hughes on a very frequent basis. For some 13 months, in fact, I was with Hughes more than any other person on the face of the earth. My job classification was "bodyguard." I'd like to have you think that I performed the typical duties of a guard—protecting Hughes from the outside world; accompanying him on his missions of worldly importance; protecting him and his wife from those who would do him harm. Well, that's what I'd like to have you think. Actually, I was nothing more than a damned baby-sitter. That's really all it amounted to: I was a baby-sitter for a 52-year-old multimillionaire. (He didn't become a billionaire until after I'd quit.) It was during this period that Hughes stopped appearing in public. He rarely left his hotel suite, never had any visitors (unless you count me, the other bodyguards and staff permitted to enter his room, and some waiters who brought his food), and, as far as I knew, never had any serious plots made against his life. (He *was* once menaced by a man with a gun, a story I'll get to later.)

It was unbelievably dull work. It was also unbelievably *different.* You will find that there are some very *odd* things that happen when one is associated with Howard Hughes. You will look at him in his living room, his bedroom, his dining room, and also his favorite room, his bathroom. If you pay strict attention, you may be able to pattern your life after this common, ordinary, run-of-the-mill, reclusive, super-rich eccentric.

I can't tell you about the inner workings of the Hughes corporate empire. I wasn't privy to that kind of detailed, complicated information, except as I overheard Hughes's phone calls or took memos during the TWA crisis. I don't know whether Hughes ever met with the head of the CIA, but I can damned well think of a lot of reasons—mostly in the area of hygiene—why the head of the CIA wouldn't have *wanted* to meet with Howard Hughes.

Given the kinds of things you've heard about the kinds of people who work for Hughes, you're probably wondering how someone winds up with a job like mine, working for a man like Hughes. It happened like this.

Chapter 1

I was born January 31, 1926, in the small Colorado town of Monte Vista, a farming community in the San Luis Valley, about 280 miles southwest of Denver. The principal crop in the area, which has been economically depressed since about 1918, is potatoes.

My parents were extremely poor. During the twenties my dad decided to atone for his German blood by devoting himself to the Colorado National Guard, which meant that my mother had to support the family (I had two older brothers) by running a greenhouse. During the thirties, in the wintertime, we had what you might have thought was an unhealthy interest in the obituary columns of the local paper: only the bereaved could be counted on to buy flowers—or barter for them.

I loafed through the public schools of Monte Vista, devoting most of my energies to the result of my being small in stature and big of mouth: I got into a lot of fights. I also was pretty good at football, basketball (this was the dark age of the sport, when you could play without being six feet or more), baseball, and track. I was also pretty good at the pool table. In short, I was just another well-rounded, small-town American boy.

In 1944 my dad was offered a good job in Van Nuys, California. An old friend of his from Colorado had made a lot of money as a contractor in the Los Angeles area, and he called my dad and offered him some work. Dad left almost without hanging up the phone, and my mother and I followed soon after. (My older brothers were already in the service.)

It was frightening to move from a town that had 3,500 residents to a suburb of L.A. in which my new high school had 3,500 *students*. My smoking on school grounds got me thrown out of Van Nuys High, and I bounced back to Colorado to try and get a diploma but my big mouth got me thrown out of school just before graduation.

That meant there was nothing between me and the armed services, and I wound up in the navy. Since I couldn't learn to shut up, I spent a lot of time cleaning up after other people, but I was finally trained as a gunner's mate. Naturally, when I was shipped overseas, I wound up with a shore-based outfit, a fleet recreation center. It was located at Osmena Beach, on the island of Samar, in the Philippines. The base was supposed to provide recreational facilities for the ship-based crews of much of the U.S. Navy in the Pacific.

The primary facility we maintained there was an inventory of around 120,000 cases of beer, kept in huge walk-in refrigerators. Each sailor who came ashore was given a chit enabling him to buy two cans or bottles for $.15. The beer was consumed in a beer hall that accommodated around 3,000 people; it was also the scene of a stunning array of gambling concessions that were run by the shore personnel: craps, blackjack, poker, a cock-fighting ring, and some shell-and-pea games. Our people simply cut the pots, and some got rich doing it.

Technically, we were all supposed to be on shore patrol when liberty parties were ashore. But that would have conflicted with the gambling duty we were pulling, and it would have put us in the middle of some of the biggest fights I ever hope to see: battleship crew against battleship crew, destroyer against destroyer, carrier against carrier. The first time I saw 200 men slugging it out I hid my shore patrol armband and billy club under my mattress.

Late in 1945 we were told that the base was being closed. I was sent to a naval supply depot about 60 miles away. It was horrible! There were inspections, roll calls, and all the normal military duties that we hadn't had at my previous station. I was assigned to the motor pool and then hooked onto the base newspaper, figuring that that duty beat changing sparkplugs on Jeeps. At first I was the mimeo operator, and when I proved I couldn't run the machine, I became a reporter. Three months later the editor was shipped home and I took his job. The one thing you could say about the papers I edited was that they came out on time.

In 1946 I was discharged and arrived in L.A. like the rest of the vets—out of work and with some peculiar skills (in my case, part-bartender, part-journalist, part-gunner's mate, mostly a goof-off). I enrolled in Los Angeles City College, hoping to become an accountant. But because the place was swamped with vets, I ended up with classes that no one else wanted, mostly in the English department.

I was also spending a lot of time playing semipro football, and softball, and it was during a softball game that I met a tall, athletic, good-looking woman named Virgie. I courted her for three years until her stern Italian father finally learned to accept me and my aversion to lasagna.

We were married in 1949, had four children in five years, and then I had a pioneering vasectomy.

To support the family I had bought a newsstand along the side of a building at the corner of Sepulveda and Ventura blvds. It was a 15-hour-a-day, 7-days-a-week job, and I soon found myself working for a major dairy, Golden State, delivering milk house-to-house. It wasn't much better than peddling papers, so I moved up. I went to work for another dairy, delivering milk wholesale—store-to-store. It paid fairly well, and I stayed with it for five years. Then I was hired by Kraft Foods as a salesman. I got my own car, got to wear a suit, had an expense account, and didn't have to punch in or out. That was my undoing: I thought the company didn't care what I was up to, which was selling a *lot* of product. When an executive of Kraft complimented me on the job I was doing—which was taking orders by phone and playing a lot of golf—I blew up and quit. What I wanted was a vice-presidency, not compliments. I had been there one week less than five years. My obligations were a wife, four kids, a new house, a car I was paying off, a sick dog, and a lot of bills.

Chapter 2

The year was 1957; there was a minor recession going on. Bright-eyed, honest, intelligent, and eager young salesmen were a dime a dozen. I began to get worried. I busted my ass every day to see if I could get a decent job, but there was nobody who would even give me a ray of hope. I was ready to take the gas pipe when I ran into my good old buddy Dick Homer, whom I had met at the pool hall. His employment history was not too far different from mine, so he fully understood my plight. I had known for a long time that Dick had a side job that caused him to work a lot of evenings and most weekends, in addition to his regular job as an optical-frame salesman. I never knew for whom he worked on the side or what the job consisted of—just that he moonlighted. He told me he felt he could get me on the payroll at this place, but that I would have to work some strange hours and that the work wouldn't be anything to write home about. At least it would be a job, and I could put some bread on the table. I was ready to do anything at that time, and I figured that Dick wouldn't steer me wrong. He had graduated from Van Nuys High School with my wife-to-be and gone into the army. A Mormon, he had graduated from Brigham Young University, had married a woman he had met there, had four kids, and was one hell of a nice guy. That's all I knew. Dick told me he would see what he could do in my behalf and that I might be hearing from someone in the near future.

A couple of days went by before I was contacted. My phone rang and the caller identified himself as Bennie Carlisle. He said that Dick had told him about me and that he would like to talk to me. I anticipated a formal interview with a scheduled time and was surprised to find that Bennie wanted to meet me within the next 30 minutes. He asked me to meet him at a Standard service station at the corner of Victory Boulevard and Balboa Avenue in the western section of Van Nuys. This seemed strange to me and I wanted to make sure I had the story straight. "You say that you want me to meet you at the Standard station at the corner of Victory and Balboa?" He replied, "That's right." "You want me to be there within the next thirty minutes?" "Uh-huh." I had the time right, too. I had decided that the whole thing must be for real and was determined to make a good impression. "I'll be delighted to meet you—how will I know you?" He answered, "I'll be sitting in a new green Chevrolet which will be parked by the telephone booth." Click.

I was left with a dead telephone in my hand. I had been doing yardwork since early morning and hadn't been too tidy when the phone rang. I now had about ten minutes in which to get spruced up for my interview. I chose to take a quick shower and an unusually quick shave and found that I didn't have enough time to get dressed up. I threw on a clean polo shirt, some clean Bermuda shorts, and my sandals and was heading out the door with barely enough time to make the ten-minute drive to the station. When I got there I was disappointed to see that there was no green Chevrolet parked by the telephone booth. I pulled into the station and drove around the building to make sure I hadn't overlooked the car. It wasn't there. I made a quick tour of the neighborhood to see if the other party had perhaps parked nearby. No luck. I pulled alongside the curb and parked my car next to the phone booth. My frustration grew as I checked my watch and found that it was 15 minutes past our meeting time.

I was cursing my luck—I just knew I had blown my opportunity—when I saw a blue Chevrolet pull into the parking area and park alongside the telephone booth. I quickly reviewed my previous conversation . . . he had definitely said he would be driving a *green* Chevrolet . . . but there was a guy sitting in a *blue* Chevrolet. At this point I felt I didn't have a hell of a lot to lose, so I got out of my car and walked over to the blue Chevy. "Are you Mr. Carlisle?" He looked at me in a very casual manner and said, "Call me Ben." I stood at the side of the car until he said, "Go around to the other side and get in." I did. When I was inside, he produced a folded piece of paper from his shirt pocket, handed it to me, and said, "Fill this out." It was a standard, short-form employment application. I had filled out 50 of them in the previous three weeks as I made the rounds. I wrote in all of the blank places on the form, keeping things very low key. (Sometimes—well, quite often—I am guilty of throwing a little bullshit into the facts I list on an employment application.)

He took the form from me, glanced at it, and said, "Do you know where Clover Field is?" When I replied that I didn't, he proceeded to give me instructions on how to find it. About halfway through his conversation it dawned on me that he was talking about an airfield I had always known as Douglas Airport—well, at least it's next to Douglas Aircraft Company in Santa Monica. Ben continued, "You will have to report to the southeast corner of that airport. Be there just before midnight. There is a car parked there near a Convair 440. Tell the guy who is in the car that you are relieving him and he will tell you what to do." He looked at me with his soulful eyes and that seemed to indicate that our discussion was over. I said, "Thanks a lot. I'll try to do a good job for you." I was getting out of the car as I said this and he was starting the motor. I stood and watched as he drove away and then got in my car and drove home. There, I grabbed a beer and went outside to join my wife, who was sitting on the lawn with a couple of her neighborhood ladies—the local kaffeeklatsch.

"Honey, I got a job. I start at midnight tonight." She let out a minor whoop and in an excited voice said, "Gee, that's great. Who are you going to work for?" That question would have been bad enough if my wife and I had been alone, but there were two other gals sitting with us, with their big ears hanging out. I could only say, "I'll tell you later," as I took my beer and went into the house. It didn't take her long to join me. "Who is the new boss, honey?" I weakly replied, "I don't know." She seemed puzzled by the answer but continued the questions: "How much are you going to make?" She was deserving of much better, but I gave her the only answer that I had: "I don't know." I wasn't doing too much for her peace of mind, but she wanted to share in my life and felt she could best do so by showing curiosity about my new way of life. When she said, "What are you going to be doing?" I knew I was trapped. One more time: "I don't know." Now my wife is not ordinarily given to profanity in daily speech, but when she said, *"SHIT!"* on her way out the door, I knew what she meant.

I grabbed another beer and headed for the back yard —my wife had gone into the front yard, and I was not too anxious to have her ask me any more questions. I sat in a chaise longue and started asking myself some questions. Since Virgie had done such a good job, I started with hers: Whom was I going to work for? What would I be paid? What would I be doing? This was the very first time I'd ever taken a job without having all of this information firmly resolved. Of course this was the first time I'd ever been interviewed in a Chevrolet . . . wearing Bermuda shorts . . . with a half-hour's notice . . . by a guy driving a wrong-colored Chevy. I thought about it during my next few beers and could find solace only in the one obvious factor—the whole goddamned thing was *weird!* But I wasn't going to let anything stand in my way. I needed a job and now I had one . . . for whomever . . . doing whatever . . . for how much. I made a mental resolve to go to the airport early the first night. I wanted to be extra sure I had some time to spend with the guy I was going to relieve. I had a bunch of questions to ask him.

I left the house at 10:30 P.M. and was at Clover Field by 11:00. It was shortly after 11:00 when I found the section of the airport I wanted, saw a Convair 440 parked there, and finally saw a filthy Chevy on the west side of the aircraft. I parked my car and walked over to the Chevy. It was empty. I wasn't upset at the moment—I didn't know what the guy in the car was supposed to be doing, so I just naturally felt that he was somewhere else doing it. I figured he would be returning to the car before his quitting time at midnight. Ben Carlisle had told me to get my instructions from the guy, so I knew I would be seeing him soon. I sat on a fender of the Chevy and waited.

As I waited patiently for my counterpart's arrival, I took advantage of the opportunity to acquaint myself with the physical layout of our sector. The biggest thing I could see in the dim light was a Convair 440. A Convair 440 is a twin-engine aircraft that looks a lot like the old Douglas DC-3. This particular aircraft looked like it had been there for 90 years. There was an accumulation of dust on the wings and fuselage that seemed to be three inches thick. The neighborhood birds had adopted the tip of the rudder as their commode, and there was a string of old birdshit running down the rudder forming a triangle about 1 inch wide at the top and probably 8 inches wide at the bottom, with a depth from a minimum of ½ inch at the top to 2½ inches at the bottom. There was probably enough birdshit on the tail of the plane to enhance the growth of over 225 plants. The tires were pudgy-looking from loss of air, and there was a dark outline under each engine that looked as if it had come from oil leaks. It was not an aircraft that would be featured on the cover of any of the airplane periodicals. There were stakes, with rope eyes, attached in the general outline of the airplane and some 20 feet past the extremities. The rope was in place in some of the areas, but was sagging to the ground or totally missing in most of the sections. The Convair seemed to have that section of the airport to itself.

As I conducted this geographical survey I had repeatedly checked my watch. I had seen the time pass from 11:15 to 11:50 and still had not seen the person I was going to relieve. This pissed me off, because I'd gone out of my way to get there early so I could receive my instructions and get some answers to my questions. At 12:00 I was more than a little bit pissed off, and, surprisingly, just a little bit scared. I have never had a job where you weren't taken by the hand, introduced to your coworkers, given an outline of your duties, had the washroom pointed out, and in general been told of the procedures. Now I was in a remote place in a very desolate airfield, had not seen my fellow employee, had no idea as to what I was supposed to be doing—and worse—I still didn't know who I was working for.

There was a cool breeze blowing in off the Pacific Ocean, and it had turned a little chilly. I decided to wait in the car for the eventual return of the other person. As I slid in behind the wheel I noticed a large piece of paper that had been stuck under the horn ring on the steering wheel. I turned on the dome light and read: "My wife has not been feeling well. I had to leave a little early." It was signed, "Parker," and had the numbers 11:45, which I took to be the time of the correspondence. Well, that really blew my cool, because if he had left that note at 11:45 he would have had to push me out of the way to leave the car.

I would just have to make the best of a bad situation. I was upset at not having been able to talk to the guy, but if his wife was sick and he wanted to be with her, it was a semi-legitimate excuse. I spent the remainder of the night in a straight-up position, sitting in the car with my eyes riveted on the Convair. I didn't know what I was supposed to be watching for or what I was supposed to do if I saw anything, but I didn't let that deter me. I watched. I watched until my eyes hurt, and then I did a grievous thing: I closed my eyes for a short moment—and fell asleep. I had no idea how long I slept, but I woke with a start—all four times that I woke up.

I had not been prepared to start work so quickly, particularly on the graveyard shift, particularly after a day of working in my yard, so naturally I was exhausted. I died a million deaths each time I awoke from one of those short naps. My first action was to check to see that the Convair was still where it was when I last saw it. It never disappointed me; it was always sitting in the same spot. I would then give the area a very sharp visual inspection to see if there were any figures lurking in the shadows. There weren't. Then I would get out of the car and make a complete circle around it—even looking underneath— to make sure that some stealthy footpad hadn't snuck up on the car while I was asleep. That hadn't happened.

I was very glad to see the sun come up. That meant I had made it through the dangerous night hours. The only bad part about the sunlight came from being able to see the Convair clearly. If I had thought it looked like a dirty mess in the moonlight, I was about one-tenth right. It was the dirtiest, crummiest, ugliest-looking piece of hardware I'd ever seen. The Chevy I had slept in ran a close second. The birdshit—in moonlight—was gross, but in broad daylight it was even worse because you could see it in all its technicolor glory. There were indeed oil drippings under the engines, huge black globs of gunk. The protective ropes that served to protect the perimeter of the plane looked obscenely inefficient. The total image, at least to my eyes, was that this plane had been parked there by Pancho Villa's men—when they were drunk. I took heart in the knowledge that I would soon see my relief man drive up.

I waited for 8:00—nobody showed; 8:30—nobody; 9:00—still nobody. By now I was exhausted . . . and frustrated . . . *and* mad . . . *and* hungry . . . *and* disillusioned. So I went home. If my relief man came and found that I wasn't there, that was just going to be too goddamned bad. I wasn't even convinced that I was on anybody's payroll. I thought I was the victim of a gigantic put-on.

I was more than a little bit irritated as I drove to my home. Now you know what happened the instant I walked into the house? My wife was seated at the dining-room table, along with three of the neighbors, and was already poised to ask the question: "Hi honey, how did it go?" Now I loved this gal very, very much and if it was at all possible I was going to give her an answer that would put her mind at ease. I knew that if I answered the first question, I would have to field the other three—"Who do you work for? . . . What do you do? . . . How much do you make?" She needed the answers, not only for herself, but to shut up the neighbors, who had been bugging her since our initial conversation the previous day. I couldn't answer any of these questions, and no-body knew it any better than I. So I did the expedient thing: I said *"Shit!"* and went to bed. I didn't fall asleep, mind you. It was going to be a while before I could go to sleep right after I'd gone to bed.

Chapter 3

I spent a few fitful hours in bed, but found that I was unable to sleep for over fifteen minutes at a time. The same questions kept pounding through my head: Who am I working for? What am I supposed to be doing? How much am I being paid? I wanted desperately to get the answers to these questions, not only for my own good but to satisfy my wife's curiosity. Around midday I had a sudden brainstorm and headed for the telephone. I would call my friend Dick and ask him for these answers. He would undoubtedly know since he had got me the job. I dialed his number and his wife answered. I hurriedly said, "Hi, Jo. This is Ron. May I speak to Dick?" All of the pieces would soon be made to fit.

She replied, "Dick is in Bakersfield for the week and won't be back until Friday evening." I damned near broke into tears. I asked her if she knew where he would be staying. She had no idea. I asked her if she expected to hear from him. No—he never called unless he was going to be out of town over the weekend. There was precious little hope of getting in touch with him before he returned on Friday. I tried to conceal my disappointment and made routine inquiries into her health, the health of her children, and so on. I fought off the desire to unload my problem on her. I was afraid she would take a reasonable point of view and tell me I was stupid to have accepted a job with all the unknowns this one had. Fishing, I casually mentioned that through Dick's influence I had been able to go to work for the company that Dick moonlighted for. Not biting, she said simply, "That's nice." I said good-bye and hung up.

Grabbing a can of beer from the icebox, I went out to the patio for some self-analysis. I had been sitting and thinking for quite a while when I made a sudden discovery. My family wasn't home. The kids had been out of school a few hours and I hadn't noticed that they weren't around. The car was gone; so was Virgie. Nobody was there but me and Aggie, the dog. Needing another beer to think on, I went to the kitchen. Then I saw it, a large note lying on the counter. Judging from the 2:30 time on it, it had been there for the past five hours. It said, "Will be home in time for you to go to your job." She had underlined *job,* and I thought that she had managed to make the line rather cruel in appearance. There was no greeting, no closing, no signature. Obviously it was from a very mad, very disgusted wife. I heated up a box of Kraft macaroni and cheese marked FOR SAMPLE USE ONLY and sat in the darkened living room. The dinner formed a one-pound lump in my stomach as I sat and tried to figure out my new lot in life. I spent hours that night feeling extremely sorry for myself.

The family returned at 9:00 P.M. It was not a festive homecoming scene. The kids seemed to have taken the side of their mother in the strained relationship; they didn't bother to kiss me good-night for the first time in their lives.

I made a bologna sandwich and threw it into a paper

bag along with some potato chips and cookies I stole from the kids' lunch boxes. I took a quart thermos bottle, which I intended to have filled with coffee at the first restaurant I passed.

It was barely 10:00 P.M. as I headed over the Sepulveda Pass, going from the San Fernando Valley into the Los Angeles basin. I *knew* I would be able to meet Parker, or whoever the other guard was, by arriving at my duty-post a full hour and a half before I was scheduled to be there. Everything looked the same as I parked my station wagon in the lot at the airport. Everything *was* the same except for the note inside the Chevy. It now read, "Wife isn't feeling any better. Had to leave a little early. Parker." It bore the time 11:37. I looked at my watch: 10:26. I had checked my watch against a radio station as I drove from home, so I made a mental note to check with Parker, if and when I ever met him, to find out if we were in the same time zone or if he was on double daylight savings, or what.

As long as I was already there, I figured that I might as well go to work. That night it consisted of me sitting and wondering just what in hell I was doing there. I had my sandwich at 2:00 A.M. and was able to stay awake almost all night without the coffee I had forgotten to stop and get. The Kraft dinner and the sandwich were jostling for position in my stomach, and they kept me awake to referee.

My target was 8:00 A.M., when my relief man would, I hoped, show up. It was a replay of the previous morning. He never arrived, and I went home at 9:00.

When I got home I wasn't at all surprised to find another note. "I've gone" was all it said. I wondered how Virgie had managed to get away so easily since it was early, she hadn't had the car or any money, and there were no nearby buses. I knew I couldn't sleep, so I spent the day doing yard work. The kids didn't come home from school at the usual time; I decided to try and overlook that fact. I had to assume that Virgie had picked them up. If she hadn't, then they were at the mercy of one of those hot items who hang around grammar schools at the age of 57.

I put the tools away, took a hot shower, shaved, took a can of beer, and went out to the patio. Suddenly I noticed that Aggie was gone, too. *That was really going too far.* If Virgie wanted to get mad at me, even if she wanted to get the kids on her side—well, I'd just have to live with that. But to take my *dog?* That was going overboard. I started to think out my argument for the upcoming battle and fell asleep.

I was awakened by the ringing of an alarm clock that had been put, mysteriously, alongside the chaise longue. It had been set for 11:15. While that didn't leave time for any exploration of my current matrimonial problems, I was happy to see that a lunch had been packed and the thermos was full of coffee. (Well, maybe she wasn't *too* mad.) I pushed the station wagon over the hill for the third night. This time the note read, "Had to go to an all-night drugstore to have a prescription filled. Parker. 11:45." At least this Parker guy was an inventive soul: he had a new excuse for every day. I was beginning to admire his style, if not his dedication.

It was a beautiful night, and I had slept during the afternoon and evening, so I did a little walking that night. I went around the perimeter of the Convair and tried to repair the rope barriers. I tied as many knots as possible, but there were places where there was no rope to tie. I kept looking around as I walked, halfway expecting someone to jump out of the airplane and confront me.

23

Finally, getting my courage together, I decided to make the big move. I walked over and stood under the nose of the Convair, listening for sounds, human or otherwise, from inside the plane. Nothing. I walked back toward the tail and held my ear against the fuselage. Not a sound. I was extremely disappointed. I had hoped that the Convair could give me some clue as to why I was watching it—if indeed the Convair was *what* I was supposed to be watching. The same fellow who hadn't relieved me the past two days didn't show up at 8:00, so I left my post at 8:01. (I may not be the brightest guy in the world, but eventually I *do* catch on.) The cold war was still on at home, but a couple of the kids said hello to me when they got home from school, and Aggie licked my hand a couple of times. It wasn't great, but it was better than the day before.

I slept from 6:00 P.M. until about 11:30. I was moving very slowly, not the least bit worried that I was going to be late at the airport. *Who would know besides me?* I took my time driving, and got there at 12:20. As I walked up to the guard car, I was astonished to see a guy sitting on the passenger side of the car. I immediately began to think of a suitable alibi, but I couldn't come up with one. I had walked up to the car and was standing by the driver's door when I was struck with a sudden realization. The man in the car hadn't seen me pull into the parking lot; he had missed me walking up to the car; and he had completely failed to notice that I was now standing about a foot from the door of the car. I pressed my face against the window to see what he was doing; to make certain he was *alive*.

The fellow was a young man of perhaps 22, clean-cut, with a lanky frame. He was almost hidden in a stack of textbooks and notepapers. He had the car's dome light on and had mounted a seven-cell flashlight to the door-frame over his right shoulder with an intricate web of rubber bands. I stayed at the window for a couple of minutes, hoping he would notice me. I was reluctant to knock on the window for fear I would startle him and he would reach under the seat, pull out a gun, and blow my head off. (I knew *I* hadn't had a gun while sitting there, but I wasn't sure but that the changing of the guard also entailed the passing of the weapon.) Finally I made my move. I tapped at the window, ready to dive under the car if that was called for. The guy looked up at me, smiled, and gestured to me to open the door and get in. I did. He shook my hand and gave a name that sounded like Pat. I told him mine and followed with a string of questions.

"Who do we work for?"

"Hughes Productions."

"What are we paid?"

"Two dollars an hour. Time and a half after forty hours."

When I asked him what we were supposed to do on this assignment, he looked at me quizzically and said, "We're supposed to see that nobody goes near that airplane." He pointed to the Convair. As we talked he was gathering up his papers and books. He opened the door, explaining, "I go to Loyola College and I've got a first-period test tomorrow. I've got to get some sleep. See you tomorrow." With that he was gone. But I felt great. I could answer those three questions for myself and for Virgie. I slept wonderfully!

I was wide-awake by 6:30 that morning, waiting for 8:00 to arrive so I could go home and talk to Virgie. Just before 8:00 a man pulled up in the parking lot and began to unload his car. He pulled out a folded chaise longue, a small insulated box, a picnic basket, and a large stack of books. He was dressed in Bermuda shorts, polo shirt, and tennis shoes. His well-tanned body gave evidence of a lot of time in the sun; for all practical purposes he looked like someone heading for the beach. But if he was my relief I *did* want to talk to him. On this day, however, I had a more pressing duty. As soon as I was sure he was coming over to my location I took off on the dead run for my station wagon. As we passed each other I said to him, "I have to run. My wife has been feeling poorly. See you later." I was in my car and halfway home before he had a chance to respond. As I drove, I kept wondering what had prompted me to offer that particular explanation for my rapid departure.

Neither my wife nor I believe in long drawn-out arguments, so it was very easy for me to get the conversation started. I told her that the new employer was Hughes Productions, that I was being paid $2.00 an hour, and that I watched an airplane at Clover Field. I also told her that there had been a mention of overtime. This was important to us because we knew we could not even begin to exist on $80.00 per week. I told her I had seen enough screwy things already to be convinced that this was a nowhere job and that it was only temporary and I would continue to look for work more suitable to my qualifications. We had a lot of fun making up.

I was at Dick's house early on Saturday morning to get him to tell me everything he knew about my new job. He told me that Hughes Productions was the nonproducing movie company owned by Howard Hughes. I had heard of Howard Hughes before—who hadn't?—and remembered that he had produced *The Outlaw* and some other movies. Dick informed me that Hughes Productions hadn't made a movie for quite a few years and that nobody seemed to know when they might ever make another one. He went on to say that there was a wide range of assignments that come forth from Operations—the control center for Hughes Productions—and that my job of guarding the airplane was quite typical of the workaday activities. He also told me that almost all the employees of Hughes Productions were Mormons, since the hiring was done by the Operations executives, who were themselves all Mormons. Dick said I was given the job on a temporary basis—he felt it was below my capabilities—and that my future would be very limited. Even if I chose to make Hughes Productions a career I would have very limited advancement since I was a non-Mormon and my life-style was about 180 degrees removed from the Mormon life-style. He thought this temporary income would allow me to feed my family while I continued to job hunt during the daylight hours; for this reason I had been given the graveyard shift. He did a lot of laughing as I told him of the frustrations I had suffered from not having contact with the mysterious Parker and the daytime replacement, who hadn't made an appearance on the first two days. When I told him of the vacationlike appearance of the daytime man he went into gales of laughter and could only gasp, "You'll get used to it." Virgie had gone with me when I talked to Dick. She was pleased to hear that both Dick and I considered the job temporary and that we were plucking money from the fabled Howard Hughes money tree, even if the harvest was coming in slowly.

After two months of airport duty—reading, sleeping, and then occasionally not showing up at all (I was learning from Parker)—I received a phone call that directed me to report to 941 North Orange Street, in Hollywood. I was to talk to a Bishop Lundeen. (His name was Howard, but Mormons always referred to him by his religious title.) I made real sure I was there at the proper time. Lundeen was from the ivory tower of Operations and seemed to be conducting a follow-up interview to the one that had taken place at the gas station. We chatted about my background, education, family status, and employment aspirations. That part of the interview seemed to go rather well, and I had the feeling that I wouldn't be fired on the spot. He then asked me if I smoked. Since I had a package of Viceroys showing through the pocket of my shirt I felt compelled to say, "Yes, I smoke." He recoiled slightly at the answer, but continued the interview. "Do you drink?" From the way he said *drink* I had the feeling I was in trouble. I wasn't about to lie about it, however, and gave him a truthful answer, "I like my beer, and I'm what is commonly called a 'social drinker,' but drinking is not a problem with me and I can take it or leave it." Shit! I'd rather look for a job than find out somebody was going to tell me I couldn't drink. The interview was terminated very shortly after that question, and I drove home with the feeling that I'd just been given a shove toward the unemployment office. My pessimism, however, was unfounded.

Operations called a couple of days after my interview with Bishop Lundeen and I was given the following message: "We have had to put Parker on another assignment. For the time being we would like to have you work two shifts at the airport. Please report for duty at 4:00 tomorrow afternoon and work until 8:00 the following day." No mention was made of days off. My mental arithmetic told me I'd be working 112 hours a week. Forty hours at $2.00 and 72 hours at $3.00 an hour. That was $296.00. Hell! I could stand a few weeks of that, especially now that I knew I could sleep most of the time. I loaded up our station wagon and reported for my first 16-hour shift. I wasn't about to stay in that crummy Chevy. I took an air mattress I had blown up and put it in the back of the wagon. (It became a little chilly the first night, so I took a sleeping bag for the rest of my double shifts.) I found that I became bored quite early and spent a lot of time in walking around the Convair. This was just as boring, and I decided to spend my time in my favorite diversion—reading. The problem was in getting enough light. I prowled around the airport and found a plug normally used by maintenance crews during the day. Then I bought 200 feet of electrical cord, ran the cord to my station wagon, and installed a reading lamp. (During the cold months I also used the cord to run an electric heater I had bought.) I read popular hardcovers, paperbacks, technical books, and any other sort of printed material I could get my hands on. I'm a fairly fast reader and it wasn't uncommon for me to read three paperbacks in the time span of a 16-hour shift.

Then reading became boring, so I turned to other diversions. I made moccasins, purses, key chains, and wallets. I became the best customer our local hobby shop had ever seen. Every close friend, and several casual acquaintances, had a handmade leather gift from old Ron. I slept enough at the airport so that when I was home I'd be wide-awake and could enjoy the family from 8:30 until 3:30. This worked pretty well for a few weeks, especially on payday, but I became bored with the unusually long hours—particularly with no days off. I called the Operations telephone number I had been given and asked that I be scheduled for an occasional day off. The return phone call notified me that I would be allowed to have a day off each week and that I would be told when it would be. I never heard from anybody to tell me which day off I should take, so I began to improvise. If I had something to do on Tuesday, that would be my day off. The same held true for Saturday, Thursday, or any other day that was convenient for me. Some weeks would contain one day off. Some would have two, and many would have as many as four days off. Now my job was *great*. My wife and I knew this was just a temporary job, but the money was so good that we decided I should milk the situation for all it was worth. Then we would be better equipped for me to do the necessary job hunting.

My phone rang at about 11:30 one night. It was Rodney, a man on the staff at Operations. I was sound asleep when the phone rang, but fortunately still had a little presence of mind. Rod said, "Ron, what are you doing at home? You're scheduled for the airport tonight." I'd been rehearsing this answer ever since I had decided not to report for duty every time I was supposed to. I said, "Oh, no I'm not. This is Wednesday and I have the day off." Would the fish take the bait? Yes: He replied, "No, this is only Tuesday and you are supposed to be there." I stammered an apology and mentioned that it was confusing to have to work six days a week and two shifts a day. Rodney expressed his regrets for my terrible schedule and then said, "There's something big happening at the airport tonight and you'd better get right over there. Remember what you have been told about your actions around Mr. Hughes and follow those instructions to the letter."

He hung up and I wondered just what the hell it was I'd been told concerning my exposure to Mr. Hughes. My pal Dick had laughingly told me of some of the far-out rules of behavior when in the presence of Howard Hughes, but I had not paid particular attention to them since they had been contained in a humorous anecdote as opposed to a law of the land. I now searched my memory for these procedures, which would help to get me through the night. To the best of my memory, the instructions were: Do not *ever* look at Mr. Hughes; do not *ever* speak to Mr. Hughes unless you are commanded to do so; do not *ever* touch Mr. Hughes or any of the people who are with him; do not *ever* allow anyone to speak to, or touch, Mr. Hughes.

It had all sounded like so much bullshit when I was hearing the story, but now it seemed to be the most important catechism I would ever hear. I wished I had paid more attention. I was pissed off at Operations for throwing me to the wolves without the protection of the bylaws. Oh, well, easy come, easy go! I kissed my wife good-bye and headed for my rendezvous with the legendary Howard Hughes.

Chapter 4

As I headed over the Sepulveda Pass for my rendezvous with Howard Hughes I began to have second thoughts about the meeting. Until this night I had found it convenient, comfortable, and even necessary to treat the whole guard detail as a lark. I had easily adopted the life-style of my fellow guards: Show up when you wanted to—if you wanted to. Sleep as much as you wanted to. Do any damned thing you wanted to do.

But as I drove along I kept thinking—*there really is a Howard Hughes.* While Rodney had not explicitly *said* that Hughes was going to be at the airport, I knew that his reference to my conduct while in the presence of Hughes was meant to be a warning of what to expect. I began to get butterflies in my stomach. Hughes couldn't be a damned idiot and accumulate all those millions. Maybe he was a real tyrant and expected his employees—yes, even his airplane guards—to be alert, responsible, and dedicated to duty. I felt that I would be under his personal inspection, and I wanted to measure up to his standards. But I didn't know what those standards *were,* and I felt that I risked looking like a buffoon.

I stopped at a gas station and went over to the pay

phone, dialing Operations. Rodney answered.

"Rodney, I need some more information before I get to the airport."

His idea of information? "Ron, you'd better hurry up and get to the airport. If you're not there, we could all get in trouble."

I didn't need that kind of advice and said so: "Rodney, I'm damned near there, but I don't know what the hell I'm supposed to do when I *get* there."

His voice went up an octave or so. "What do you *mean* you don't know what to do?"

The futility of trying to explain the situation was obvious. Anything I said that approximated the truth could (and probably would) be used against me and the other guards. I could wreck a lazy man's paradise. "Rod, just tell me what to do when I'm around Hughes."

He chanted out some instructions. "Don't look at Mr. Hughes. Don't talk to Mr. Hughes. Don't touch Mr. Hughes . . ." The words seemed to run together; they all sounded the same. I could tell from his voice that Rodney was sharing a sense of frustration and was giving me as much help as he could. But it still wasn't doing much to solve the problem. I felt like a guy who was getting his first swimming lesson after his boat had sunk five miles from shore.

"Well, for Christ's sake, at least tell me what Hughes *looks like* so I'll know who not to look at!" It seemed a simple request.

"I've never seen him," blurted Rodney. *That* surprised me. I figured that all the Operations crew would be in constant touch with Hughes. It seemed impossible that Rodney hadn't ever seen the boss.

Feeling totally lost, I hung up the phone and got back in the station wagon. Rodney had still been talking when

33

I slammed down the receiver. The question, though, was whether to continue south and risk looking like an ass in front of Howard Hughes, or go north, back to my home and ultimately the unemployment office. I consider it a tribute to my character that I headed south.

As I pulled into the airport parking lot I was happy to see that there wasn't a lot of activity around the Convair. I parked my station wagon, since I felt it was mandatory on this one night to sit in the company car while performing my guard duties. As I walked over to the company car I saw a van—sort of like a United Parcel truck—parked under the far wing of the plane. It had been hidden from me as I drove up. There were six men standing around the van busily chatting among themselves. I fought off the desire to walk over to them and find out what they were doing there. (On the one hand, they might be the marauders I had been more-or-less guarding against, come at last. On the other hand, one of them might be Howard Hughes, and I would have broken rule number one: Don't look at Howard Hughes.)

I got into the company car and prepared to assume the position of airplane guard, but it wasn't going to be that simple. I hadn't been inside that car for so long that I had forgotten the most important fact about it: it had sat idle for so long, had been unused for such a long time that it had accumulated so much grime on the windows that it was impossible to see out of the damned thing. I grabbed an old newspaper from the back seat, got out of the car, and started wiping the dirt from the window— no easy task. After about five minutes of anxious scrubbing I had managed to get the windshield, as well as the windows for the two front doors, relatively clean. As I was wiping, I heard the sounds of laughter coming from the men standing by the plane; I figured they were laughing at me, and I was embarrassed as hell.

More than embarrassed, in fact—I was shook up. For example, I started to light a cigarette a couple of times but didn't complete the act. I wasn't sure *why* I wasn't lighting up, except that it seemed wrong to smoke on guard duty with the boss coming. So I just sat there and waited.

It was a dark night. I was about 50 yards from the group of men at the van and could see them by outline only. I rolled the window down in hopes of being able to hear their conversation, but the distance was too great. I could hear some laughter from time to time; it seemed they were enjoying themselves. They were obviously waiting for someone, and it seemed logical to me that they must be waiting for Howard Hughes. I was surprised to see that some of the men were smoking. I could see matches being lit and the glow of cigarettes as I watched them. I joined in—what the hell—if those guys weren't afraid to smoke with Hughes about to arrive, I wouldn't be either.

The relaxed attitude of the six men had served to take some of the pressure off me, and I had shaken off some of my tension. It was after 1:00 A.M. and there was very little traffic on Bundy Drive, which ran along the east side of the airport. I watched the occasional cars as they drove along so that I would be alert to any that turned onto the airport road. I paid strict attention for about an hour and then I became bored. Old habits are hard to break, and I found myself trying to catch a little nap. I got out of the car and walked around it every now and then to help me stay awake. It was going to be a long night.

Sitting inside the car, my thoughts drifting, I caught sight of a car driving past me. It was a middle-line Chevrolet, the standard Hughes vehicle. This one was a four-door model, blue, and was occupied by the driver and one passenger, who sat in the back seat. The car pulled alongside the group of men, and the passenger opened the door and stepped out. I couldn't believe my eyes. Not a one of those six men turned their back to the car. They all stood there and looked directly at the new arrival. The group was standing in the light of the automobile, and I could see the man fairly well. He seemed to be around 6′3″ and relatively thin. He was dressed in a sport coat, a white shirt that was open at the neck, and a pair of tan slacks that seemed to be too large. He walked over to the window of the driver's side and stood talking to the driver. As he walked back to the group of men, the car made a U-turn and drove back past my location. Another U-turn brought Hughes's car to a position some 25 yards to the left of mine. That's where it stopped. The lights were turned off and the driver remained behind the wheel. I looked at the driver, but he wasn't about to return the greeting. I wondered if I was expected to walk over to the car and introduce myself. This didn't seem called for, and I decided that if anyone wanted to talk to me for any reason, they could do so at my car. It was my post and I was going to man it.

After the momentary distraction of watching the movement of the car, I turned to look at the group of men. They had disappeared. Instant panic. Where in the hell had they gone so quickly? I checked the area and could find no sign of them. I kept looking and was rewarded by sighting the van—it was clear over on the north side of the runway and was heading for the buildings that housed Douglas Aircraft. Five men, including the late arrival I took to be Hughes, were walking behind the van. I wouldn't be bothered by them for quite some time.

I kept hoping the driver of the other car would come over and let me know what was expected of me. It didn't happen. I kept stealing glances in his direction but couldn't tell if he was asleep or awake, if he was looking at me or not—he just sat behind the wheel and didn't move.

The object of the night's activity was a Douglas DC-6 cargo plane. This was a brand-new aircraft and had apparently been purchased by Hughes. (Intercompany gossip would circulate later that the reason for purchasing a cargo plane was that it didn't have windows—a passenger would not be able to look out and therefore would have no idea where he was). This plane had been painted with the identification of an air-freight company that had been unable to take delivery. You might know that a Hughes-owned plane would use an alias.

The idea was to move the DC-6 near the Convair. The distance between the hangar and the Convair was less than a half mile and was covered with asphalt macadam. Before the DC-6 would eventually be moved, though, this distance would seem more like ten miles and the terrain would become as forbidding as the Sahara Desert. Hughes had designed a tow bar that was held together by soft metal shear pins. The purpose of the special tow bar was to keep pressure off the nosewheel—I never learned why—but still allow the tow motor to be able to move the aircraft. From my position near the Convair I watched as the tow motor started slowly forward, gradually increasing its speed until it was roaring along at about two miles an hour. Even at that low speed it was impossible to cover more than 50 yards before the shear pins were severed, causing the tow bar to pull apart. This was accompanied by a loud *bang!* at the time of separation and then by the cursing of the airplane crew. Each time the tow bar separated with a *bang!-curse!* it was necessary to fit the sections together, realign the pin holes, and insert new shear pins, a procedure that had to be accomplished by flashlight.

All of this was done under the careful scrutiny of Hughes, who walked alongside the tow bar throughout the entire night. Any pebble, undulation, or crack in the pavement became an enemy because any of those things would cause an immediate separation of the tow bar. Eight hours, countless shear pins, and dozens of temper displays were used up before the DC-6 was parked alongside the Convair. Since my duty station was adjacent to the Convair, it was obvious that Hughes would be coming fairly close to where I sat. My first summit decision was rapidly approaching. My duty was to watch the Convair at all times—but Hughes was going to be standing next to the plane, and I wasn't supposed to look at him. I thought murderous thoughts about the Operations' personnel who had let me get caught in this trap without issuing me proper instructions. (This was to be the first of a hundred such occurrences.)

The first light of dawn began to illuminate the area as the DC-6 crept toward its new home. Hughes was looming larger and larger, but I had decided to keep my eyes on the old Convair and on anything else that entered that area. If this displeased Hughes, I was sure he'd let me know immediately.

My problems were magnified a hundredfold by something so ordinary that I hadn't even thought it would be a problem, much less noticed it when I was on guard duty. Clover Field Airport is and was heavily trafficked by commuter aircraft—small, private planes that are flown in by businessmen who can afford to escape the murderous freeways. There were numerous landings as dawn broke that morning. Most of these planes were to be parked within 100 yards of our immediate area. More important, the automobile parking lot was only 25 yards behind my location. We had begun to draw a sizable crowd.

It was only natural that people's curiosity would be aroused on seeing a six-man crew, plus foreman in the person of Howard Hughes, doing a two-man job. Ten or 15 early-arriving pilots moved closer to the scene to get a good look. My original instructions, remember, had been to "Keep any and all people and/or animals away from the roped-off area around the Convair." Those tattered ropes would, I knew, offer little resistance to the rubberneckers as they moved toward the DC-6. I threw a quick look at Hughes in hopes that he would, some-how, offer an easy solution to my problem. It was the first time I was to come into eyeball-to-eyeball contact with Howard Hughes, and I was crushed by it. He offered no guidance. In fact, there was an unmistakable look of ter-ror in his eyes. He thought the problem was *his,* and that *I* was there to solve it.

I jumped from the sanctuary of my car and ran to a position in front of the advancing group of men. I wished desperately that my 5'9", 180-pound body could have been quickly fortified by at least 6 inches and 50 pounds.

"Stop! Stop right where you are!" I shouted. It had a momentary effect—some of the men paused—but I could see that most of them weren't too damned im-pressed by me. There was a mutter of answers, among them, "What's wrong with *him?*" "Who's the nut?" "Got a problem, sonny?" "Get out of the way!" There were also some vulgar terms I chose not to hear.

In desperation I said, "I must ask that you not go past the roped-off area." That request would have been a helluva lot more impressive if the rope hadn't been missing from the area in which they and I were standing.

My voice had reached near high-C as a result of a sudden throat condition, but I rambled on. "The area around the Convair is leased by my company and we cannot allow you to pass over that section of ground. There really isn't anything worth seeing over there—we're just moving an airplane—so I'd like to ask all of you to go about your business and let us do the same."

For a moment I thought I'd won the battle, but then a voice from the rear of the crowd asked, "Who's the old gent in the sport coat?" As I fumbled for an answer another voice rang out, "Isn't that *Howard Hughes?*"

I could have died! There I was, completely outnumbered, with no battle plan, no relief in sight, and some bozo had to mention *the* name that uncovered our entire effort at secrecy. Before I could invent another answer, another voice boomed out, "Hell, yes! That's old Howard! I've seen him fly in and out of here for ten years."

That comment seemed to satisfy all the men. After a short discussion, they turned and made their way to the parking lot. I almost crumpled with relief, but as I looked to Hughes for what I thought would be a friendly wave or a thumbs-up signal for my good efforts, his panic-stricken eyes directed me to a new emergency.

While I had been spending my time dealing with the small crowd on the parking-lot side, a veritable mob had formed at the rear of the plane and was now rapidly approaching the work crew. As I ran to meet this new challenge I caught a glimpse of Hughes's car driving rapidly to the spot where Hughes was standing frantically waving his arms. I confronted this new group with more asinine directions, but didn't do a hell of a lot to deter them from their chosen path. As I halted the movement on the east side of the pack, I'd lose control on the west side. For the next couple of minutes I looked like a sheep dog on amphetamines. I ran back and forth, and side to side, to keep an imaginary border—losing ground with each trip until there was barely ten yards between the mob and the DC-6.

I was saved by the bell. Most of the men in this group were mechanics and other ground personnel from the airport who had been early for work. At 8:00 A.M. the crowd disappeared as quickly as it had formed. At 8:01 there wasn't a single outsider within a hundred yards of our "secret" position. With the danger past, I remembered seeing Hughes getting into his car and leaving the scene—no doubt to call Operations to inform them to get my final pay ready. I thought I might as well get my personal belongings out of the company car and get ready to head home.

As I turned around I damned near fell over the hood of the blue Chevy that contained Hughes and his driver. Feeling I had nothing further to lose, I kept on my track and walked toward the guard car. Hughes's driver sat impassively in the front seat of their car. If he had any sympathy for me he did a damned good job of hiding it. Hughes was sitting in the back seat; we were less than five feet from each other. My eyes would not be diverted. By God, I was going to take a good look, since I figured it would be my last. Much to my surprise I caught Howard Hughes looking directly at me, and, more importantly, his angular face was in the beginning stages of a grin; then he gave me a full smile.

I was to wonder about that smile for a long time. In movies about the Roman Empire it had always seemed to me that the emperor smiled as he gave the thumbs-down signal to the gladiator, who then killed the fallen foe. A few days went by and I wasn't fired. In fact, my responsibilities had doubled—I now had two airplanes to watch—and there hadn't been any criticism from Operations. My schedule remained the same; most days I worked two shifts. The extra hours had almost doubled the size of my bank account.

Chapter 5

A couple of weeks later I got a call from Kay Glenn, the head of Operations for Hughes Productions. Speaking from his office at 7000 Romaine Street in Hollywood, he told me that I had been selected to join the drivers' pool and that not only would my duties be important of themselves, but they would also ensure a better future for me with Hughes Productions.

When I reported to the drivers' room I found that I would be under the supervision of Ben Carlisle. It was nice to see him in the comfortable environs of his small office after thinking that he was forced to work out of automobiles. Ben took me aside and gave me a lengthy list of do's and don'ts that would be my guidelines for personal conduct while working as a Hughes driver. (I was starting to see a pattern develop: every important rule of the Hughes organization that was relayed to me was always transmitted verbally. I never saw any of the supposedly vital instructions in written form.) The do's were basic: Dress neatly in a conservative suit. Keep your hair neatly trimmed. Keep your nails short and clean. Be attentive to instructions. Last, but not least, be available. ("Being available" at Hughes Productions was to mean that I would be paid for many 168-hour work weeks.) The don'ts were more specific: Don't smoke. (Ben knew of my love of Viceroys, so he whizzed past *that* rule.) Don't drink. Don't eat garlic, onions, or Roquefort dressing. Don't talk to *anyone* concerning your activities. Never ask Why. (I learned later that it was okay to ask why, but your question wouldn't be answered.)

I reported for work the following Monday morning. I had invested in a new suit, new shoes, and a fresh haircut, had trimmed my nails, gone through two bottles of Listerine to wash out any lingering trace of Sunday's beer, and had, generally speaking, cleaned up my act.

The drivers' room proved to be a small, rectangular building at 941 North Orange, next door to the Romaine headquarters. It had formerly been a film drop for a major film processor but had been converted into a combination office and dayroom. The office area was quite small, 8 feet by 15 feet, and was equipped with a large desk and two telephones. One of the phones was of the conventional type; the other was a direct line from Operations. The dayroom was large, 12 feet by 20, and had floor-to-ceiling windows on two sides; the upper half of the third side was also given over to windows. This enormous expanse of glass was covered with venetian blinds. The blinds were never opened. A Ping-Pong table occupied the center of the room. Couches and easy chairs were placed around the perimeter; they accommodated 12 or 15 bodies. There were two bookcases crammed full of dog-eared paperback books that ran the gamut from *Lady Chatterley's Lover* to some very stern religious tracts. A 20-gallon aquarium had a place of honor near the door and had been stocked with some exotic breeds of tropical fish.

The work force varied in number. On some occasions

there would be as many as twelve people on hand, while at other times there would be only one person available. Most of the drivers were young, clean-cut, and intelligent. (I use the word *intelligent* in a truly academic sense. They were also very naïve, unworldly, and small-townish in their actions and speech.) The drivers were almost exclusively of the Mormon faith. This figured, because Kay Glenn, Howard Lundeen, and the powerful Bill Gay (who had taken over from Noah Dietrich as Hughes's right-hand man)—all Mormons—did all the hiring. (Only two or three of the other drivers besides me weren't Mormons.) During the summer our work force would be flooded with students from Brigham Young University. This surplus labor brought mixed blessings —there were seldom enough assignments to go around and you might not have anything to do for two or three days, causing the time to pass slowly. On the bright side, it gave us a lot of time to play Ping-Pong. I feel certain that a team from Hughes Productions could have held its own with the Red Chinese national team.

Our Ping-Pong rules were simple: survival of the fittest. The winner kept the table but had to play all challengers. There were some highly contested matches throughout the course of a day, and the player who managed to keep the table was treated with a great deal of respect. I'd like to say that I was one of the better players, but my won-lost record would refute that. My brilliant serve couldn't make up for the other players' expertise. Among the best were, interestingly enough, two of the big shots—Howard Lundeen and Kay Glenn. Glenn and Lundeen were terrible losers, which one might not have assumed given their religious nature.

But I was having a hard time adjusting as a Gentile among the members of the Mormon faith. To take a case in point, I made no bones about smoking: it was not prohibited by my brand of Methodism. Whenever one of the drivers would spot Bishop Lundeen heading from Operations to the drivers' room, a curious thing would happen: The ashtray in front of me would suddenly contain 12 cigarettes, some lit, some smoldering. Upon seeing this, Lundeen used to roll his eyes—the cursed infidel was killing himself, so be it—and I occasionally would crack to him, "I couldn't possibly smoke *all* these, Bishop." But I think he really thought I *did* smoke them all. No good Mormon would have desecrated his body.

The duties of a driver were varied. In the course of a week I might complete the following missions: pick up the newspapers for Operations. Pick up food for Operations. Pick up ice cream for Operations. Mail letters for Operations. Pick up Mrs. Nadine Henley, the personal secretary to Howard Hughes who worked out of Operations, at her home and drive her to Operations. Drive Mrs. Henley to her home *from* Operations. Take an ex-Miss California to drama lessons. Pick up a VIP at airport. (We would meet people arriving on TWA flights—and most of the VIPs were booked into L.A. on TWA—with an honest-to-God red carpet. Somehow the airline people had arranged that the VIP's baggage would be first off, so we were often in the car, heading out of the airport, before any of the regular passengers had got off the plane.) Pick up Angela, Mrs. Howard Hughes's maid, in Pacific Palisades and drive her to the Beverly Hills Hotel, where Mrs. Hughes, better known as former movie star Jean Peters, lived in a bungalow some 50 yards from Mr. Hughes's bungalow. Take Angela from the hotel to her home, a trip requiring at least two stops at supermarkets and, quite often, stops at antique shops in West L.A. (Angela never stopped talking about her noble Russian heritage and the fact that the wrong person was the servant. The visits to the antique shops reminded her of the good years before 1917.) Take starlet to dancing class. Take another starlet to singing lessons. Take payroll records to bookkeeper's house. Pick up payroll checks at bookkeeper's house and bring them back to Operations. (The payroll bookkeeper lived at the top of Nichols Canyon, above Hollywood. It was a 30-minute round trip from Operations, one we would make at least six or eight times every week. I never did find out why she was permitted to work out of her house rather than at the Operations building.) Drive our realtor to Palm Springs.

In fact, some of the errands ordered by Operations should be recorded for posterity. Big stuff like: "Take this note to the address shown on the front of the envelope. When you arrive, go to apartment number 104. Knock on the door. When the door is answered, say nothing, but give this note to the party who has answered the door. Wait there. You will be given a package. Do not open this package, but bring it back to Operations and signal in the normal manner so that we may retrieve the package."

You might think the driver was on a secretive or important mission with those kinds of instructions, but it was seldom so. Operations quite often failed to *seal* these message envelopes, no doubt trusting in the honesty, naïveté, or just plain stupidity of the drivers from Fleabite, Utah. But an *inquisitive* driver—guess who?—would accidentally read the message. Typically: "Dear Sis, Mom told me in her last letter that she had sent you pictures of the family reunion. Would you please put them in an envelope and give them to the bearer of this letter? Say nothing to this man. I will look at the pictures and send them back to you. Love, Rod." A day or two later Operations would call and ask for another driver for an errand. He would be given an envelope and instructions to "Take this note . . ." Sis got her photos back, and God only knows what it had cost Howard Hughes to provide this personalized service for some pissant in Operations. For every service we performed for Howard Hughes, we performed five for the omnipotent (in their eyes, anyway) Operations staff.

There *were* some delightful assignments to be had. One was the squiring of the starlets who had been put under contract to Hughes Productions by Walter Kane, Hughes's personal talent scout. The girls were given a very busy schedule to follow. After they had been photographed by Christy Shepard (no nudes, but bathing-suit shots and other standard Hollywood cheesecake as well as the full range of dramatic poses), they went into the full Hughes routine. A day would start with drama lessons, swing right into dance lessons, and conclude (breathlessly?) with voice lessons. Most of these were given at the private residences of the individual instructors, which were widely scattered throughout Hollywood, Beverly Hills, and West Los Angeles. A driver would be assigned to each of the young women for the day, and it was his responsibility to make sure she was on time for all of her lessons. Since each of her sessions lasted two hours, it made for a leisurely day for the driver, with plenty of goof-off time. Several of us would meet for coffee in the morning, pool or billiards in the early afternoon, and clandestine drinks towards sundown.

Instructions had been given to us concerning our conduct when we were driving the starlets. If the girl preferred, she would be allowed to ride in the front seat, but I don't have to mention that we were cautioned to keep our hands off—absolutlee no touchee! We could make small talk about the weather, show-biz, sports, current events, and so on. But we were forbidden to tell these gals who we worked for, how long we had worked there, or what our job consisted of. We could say nothing that might have allowed them to find out that we were part of Hughes Productions. This was, presumably, part of the fabled Hughes secrecy. Luckily for whoever dreamed up this rule, most of the starlets were so damned naïve or self-centered that they wouldn't have dreamed of asking just what piece of good fortune allowed them a car and driver to go with their $175-a-week contract.

There was one other regulation peculiar to the driving of the starlets, one that gave me a belly-laugh every time I drew that duty. It went, "When you are driving a vehicle with one of the female parties as a passenger, do not, at any time, drive over a dip, swale, undulation, or other uneven surface at a speed of over two miles an hour." *Two miles an hour.* That was just about the single most ridiculous thing I had *ever* heard, so obviously I had to try to find out the reasoning behind it. Finally one of the oldest employees in the drivers' room took pity on me (I had been buttonholing everyone there), and let me in on the secret. "Ron," he said, "Hughes is a tit man. You will notice that all the gals you haul around are rather amply endowed." (Indeed. They all were big-busted, slim-hipped, around 5′3″, dark-haired, and all bore a certain resemblance to Mrs. Howard Hughes.) "Hughes has a theory that sudden bumps, such as the ones you get when you hit a dip in the road at thirty miles an hour, will cause a girl's tits to bounce. This will inevitably cause a minor breakdown in the tissue, which will lead to sagging tits." For Hughes Productions, with its ass-backwards logic, that almost sounded reasonable. But I certainly had driven long enough to know what would happen to me if I slowed to two miles an hour each time I crossed a dip, undulation, swale, or other impediment on the L.A. streets. I would get rear-ended about 20 times a day if I tried to comply with that rule. I had to weigh the danger of my—and the starlet's—whiplash against the theory of tit sag. Naturally, after I thought about it I decided to save my neck. In fact, my nature compelled me not only to bend the rule, but to beat the hell out of it. Whenever I saw a decent dip in the road I'd speed up and point the car at the deepest part of it. As we hit I'd look at my passenger's breasts to see if they were bouncing. They did in fact bounce under this sort of stimulus, sometimes twice if the dip was deep enough. But I never saw any indication of sagging, although the custom of wearing bras would have masked any sag and, I suspect, prevented injurious bounce, too.

When the sun went down is when the good life really began at Hughes Productions. We took our starlets to dinner at least twice a week. It wasn't an ordinary dinner either—we ate at Perino's or the Crystal Room of the Beverly Hills Hotel, top-drawer eateries. We could not have dinner with the starlet alone; it was compulsory that she have her parents or her agent along. This was to prevent the drivers from displaying their tremendous romantic abilities. To further prevent any sort of hanky-panky each driver was followed by a private detective. In extreme cases there was another detective assigned to watch the private detective who was watching the driver. I assumed that this was done to eliminate the likelihood of a coordinated driver-detective sexual conquest, although what the driver and detective were supposed to do with the parents is open to question. In any event, this proved to be one of the funnier aspects of my job. When I left the restaurant I would carefully note the number of cars in my caravan. I would then try to adjust my speed so that I would get my shadows caught by red lights that I had just managed to clear. We would go to movies, plays, and concerts after dinner, and I considered it only good manners not to have detectives lurking around the places of entertainment.

Another diversion we employed was referred to as break-up time. On some occasions there would be as many as four groups of Hughes people having dinner at Perino's. We were not to acknowledge the presence of our friends at any time. But we, the drivers with a sense of humor, would try to break up our buddies by using facial grimaces, sending notes, or occasionally by having someone paged. My own most effective gimmick was to have the restaurant staff page Mr. Howard Hughes. It never failed to break up all of the loyal driver force. Our charges never seemed to be the wiser for our efforts, probably because they had no idea that Mr. Howard Hughes was in complete control of their present exis-tence, and, in some cases, would control their futures. Another part of my pleasure was in knowing that as I ate $20 dinners, (this was, remember, 1957, when a $20 meal *meant* something) the streets around the parking lot of Perino's were littered with gumshoes, all trying to look inconspicuous in one of L.A.'s posher neighborhoods.

Ben, the head of the drivers' room, suddenly disap-peared. He was not missing but had simply been "sent home" by Operations. His only sin was that he had vi-sited an old friend in the hospital. The fact that he had been asked to make this visit by Mrs. Howard Hughes didn't save him from his ultimate destiny. The visit, in itself, was not anything that tragic, but the nature of his friend's illness was his undoing. The friend had hepatitis. Hepatitis and mononucleosis were definite no-no's in the Hughes organization. Everyone who has been associated with Howard Hughes has an opinion as to why these two diseases are absolutely verboten, but I have never had concrete proof that anyone's theory was better than anyone else's. (My personal observation is that *any* communicable disease—and especially diseases of the respiratory system—brings the fear of God to Howard Hughes. Hughes was extremely hard of hearing, but I will guarantee you that he could hear a cough or a sneeze from a long way off, even without his hearing aid.)

Nonetheless, we had lost our old boss; his replacement, Al Bond, was to be my personal benefactor. He was a long-time employee who had spent a considerable amount of time with the "Old Man," as he called Hughes. Bond's status in the organization was that of an untouchable, since Hughes had promised him lifetime employment. He was not a Mormon and even confessed that he liked a touch of the bubbly on occasion. We hit it off immediately, probably because of our drinking habits, and I found that I was getting the softer, more lucrative assignments. I became a fat cat for the next few weeks.

No matter how fat I was getting on the job, though, I was brought back to reality when I got home and explained to Virgie that that $20-meal at Perino's with a beautiful woman was not only a business venture of some little glamour and not much sensuality, but also a lesson in the ways of private eyes and how to shake them. Naturally, I played up the spy-counterspy aspects of the assignment and played down the cleavage.

Chapter 6

The folks ordering out the platoons of private eyes to make certain I didn't bruise any cleavage with my smoldering glances were the staff at Operations—the nerve center of Hughes Productions. (Hughes Productions, incidentally, was wholly owned by Hughes Tool Company, which was wholly owned by guess who.) While on detached duty, I had been content to accept Operations as the head office, with which I had little contact, and let it go at that.

As a driver, though, I was in much closer proximity to Operations, which meant that I was constantly having to deal with them—mostly by telephone. But there were innumerable occasions when I would make a run for staff personnel, and at these times we would establish face-to-face contact. I should qualify that a bit, since you probably imagine that as being eyeball-to-eyeball contact. When I say face to face, I mean that *my* face was at street level while the guy in Operations was leaning out of a second-story window, shouting instructions down to me. If this sounds like a scene out of Molly Goldberg or Little Italy tenement living, well, you're on the right track.

The fabled 7000 Romaine was (and is, although Operations seems to have decamped after the famous 1974 burglary that blew the CIA-Hughes connection) a building one block long, a rectangle with the long side running along Romaine, between Orange Drive and Sycamore Street. It was well-secured, with four outside doors (two on Romaine, one on Orange, and one on Sycamore) that were *never* left unlocked; and there were precious few keys to unlock those doors. Very few people outside the organization got through those locked doors—entry was strictly by appointment only—and it was necessary for one of the occupants to vouch for a visitor, *personally*, before he could be admitted. If someone had an appointment with a staff member or one of the other people who worked in the building (and these appointments were, for the most part, with prospective employees from Utah), they would be met at an outside entrance and let into the building by a third person who had been told of the meeting and had waited by the door until it could be opened with the utmost safety. For Operations, utmost safety meant that a door could be opened to an authorized visitor only after a visual check had been made of the area ensuring that there was no pedestrian traffic nor any automobiles in the vicinity, parked or moving, that contained non-Hughes personnel.

A visitor's reason for entering the building governed which door would be used and into which part of the building he would be allowed. The bottom floor was relatively vacant, with several of the small offices there used for storage. Two or three downstairs offices were used by people working on supposedly secret assignments for the Hughes organization. The grapevine, though, had it that one was occupied by a meteorologist. (None of that trusting the U. S. Weather Bureau, and if Hughes had been actively flying during this period, this guy's job might have made sense. Later the weatherman joined the staff of Brigham Young University.) Another office was given over to a man we called "The Professor," a venerable chap whose sole responsibility was to scan newspapers and magazines and clip any references to Hughes or any of his businesses. (The reading list included show-biz publications as well as business-oriented magazines such as *Forbes* and *Business Week.*) Another ground-floor office was used as a fitting room whenever a local costume designer would design clothes for a starlet in whom Howard Hughes had a special interest. One of the offices had its own outside entrance and was used by the three-man crew that was permanently assigned to effect the safety and comfort of that special starlet. (We called her "the Party," and her comfort was nicely provided for by the new Cadillac limo she was driven around in, while the other starlets had to make do with those Chevys.) The guys on this detail were in a special category—higher than a driver, lower than staff—and were supposed to be completely isolated from the drivers' room. (In practice, they would come over to play Ping-Pong.)

There were two or three walk-in safes in rooms off the hallway on the bottom floor. Each of these had the appearance of a vault—complete with a large dial in the center of the door—and were used to store valuable items, which to my personal knowledge only included a considerable number of original prints of the movies produced by Hughes when he was active in Hollywood. (After the 1973 burglary, we all learned how much more was in that building.)

The second story of the building contained the nerve center of the entire Hughes empire—Operations. The northwest (Sycamore and Romaine) corner of the second story was where everything happened. The decor of the office, which faced Romaine, was impressive—plush carpeting, paneled walls, tasteful wallpaper, and large walnut desks. It all looked expensive. The one window in the room was heavily draped. Opening off the east side of the room was a smaller, more elaborate office, the domain of Kay Glenn, the resident head of Operations. (In the Hughes pecking order, Kay was directly under Bill Gay, but Gay worked out of his home and was seldom seen at 7000 Romaine.)

There were always two or more members of the staff of Operations in their office during normal business hours. They had the responsibility of handling most of the important communications between Howard Hughes and the many business entities of the Hughes empire. Since these communications were mostly conducted by phone, it followed that they had on hand the most up-to-date equipment available from the phone company or private sources.

But that was years before the Bell System had developed most of the techniques—push-buttons, call forwarding—that enrich our lives and AT&T's treasury. So there was one quirky part of the system: the main switchboard number, handled by the men in Operations from their call directors, was OLdfield 4–2500. On each call director, however, were numbers not sequentially connected with the main number and not part of its rotary system. These private numbers had been given to various honchos in certain of the Hughes companies, so that, say, the president of TWA wouldn't have to go through the normal switchboard. He'd dial (or, more likely, have his secretary dial) a number that would light up in Operation and that the Operations staff would know was *his and his alone.* The most important of these private numbers was, of course, the one reserved for the incoming calls of Howard Hughes. Hughes would call in to get his messages exactly as anyone would call in to get messages from an answering service, but the differences between what Operations did and what a normal answering service does are incredible.

There were extensive card systems—Cardex, Rolodex, and the like—on the desks at Operations that were instantly available to the staff. These systems were programmed with a great deal of information designed quickly to acquaint the staff member with the necessary facts about most of the people who could reasonably be expected to be on the other end of the phone. Armed with this knowledge, they were able to speak intelligently to the caller and to know how to handle the call. If there were messages to be relayed, minor problems to be solved, feathers to be smoothed, these things could be handled using the information in the card system. This effectively took care of the low-level business of the Hughes empire. Important problems were directed to the proper person or office for disposition. "John Doe" calls, the nuisance calls that everyone gets, were to be handled in such a way as to discourage a second call.

The important fact was that every call was logged in the following way: everything that was said, by either party, became part of a complex record kept by the staff member. From the first hello to the final click, every word, every murmur, every pause was noted in this log, as well as inflections, tone, or any other clue to the feelings of the person on the other end. The staff managed this because they were all highly qualified secretaries. They had to be able to take dictation at a fantastic rate and to type almost as quickly.

The record of these incoming calls would be fully transcribed into a permanent log, made part of the information system. Hughes would call Operations frequently to have messages relayed to him. A quick rundown would tell him the time of the call, the name of the caller, the nature of the call, and its disposition. If Hughes wished, they would read to him the complete transcript of the call. Or if he wished to return the call, he would ask for the phone number and eventually call the party back (often, however, after requesting that Operations call first to set up a definite appointment so that the party would be immediately available when Hughes called).

If Hughes did not want to talk to someone who had asked to talk to him, he would often give elaborate instructions on how to handle the situation. Operations would frequently be told to call back and offer a suitable apology: Mr. Hughes was out of the country on a business trip; Mr. Hughes was involved in a major business transaction and wouldn't have the time to call for quite a while; Mr. Hughes was feeling poorly and had strict orders to rest for an indefinite period. These messages were always transmitted in the most diplomatic fashion, since Hughes was unusually perceptive about the nature of his callers and always seemed able to guide the staff member into a thoroughly believable bit of dialogue that would satisfy the caller.

The drivers' contact with Operations lacked all the polish of the telephone procedures that had been devised to satisfy people with whom Hughes had business. Ours was as primitive as the signaling devices used by the most backward tribe in the least-developed country in Africa, when you take into account that the wrappings—phones, cars—were just that: wrappings. A routine trip will give you the idea.

The phone would ring in the drivers' room—the direct

line from Operations—and a driver would be requested. He would get on the line and hear something like this: "I'd like to have you make a run for me. Please come around to the window." The driver would then grab a set of keys off the keyboard and would walk out into the parking lot at the rear of the drivers' building. There was always a bunch of cars there—anywhere from 5 to 15— depending on how many details we had going at the moment. The cars were all one- and two-year-old Chevrolets, generally four-door models. They weren't the top of the line, but rather midrange models, gussied up with whitewall tires and radios. Needless to say, they were not painted flashy colors, and were it not for the fact that the police agencies around L.A. bought Chrysler products for their plainclothes cars, we could have been mistaken for cops.

The driver would next drive out of the parking lot and turn right onto Orange Drive. He'd then stop at the stop sign at Willoughby, one block south, turn right, drive one block, turn right on Sycamore, drive one block, and stop at the stop sign. That was Romaine. Another right-hand turn, and pull over to the curb as close to the corner as possible. Because there was a fireplug near the corner and because people in L.A. aren't compelled to park in restricted zones, this space was almost always available. After he stopped the car, the driver would honk his horn. Two honks were considered sufficient. After honking, the driver would get out of the car and walk over to the sidewalk immediately under Operations' second-story window. The driver would keep his eyes on that window, looking for any signal that might be given.

Eventually a face would appear in the window, and the driver would then be in personal contact with a member of Operations. (Sometimes the guy who called downstairs would get involved in a lengthy phone call and might not appear for 10 or 15 minutes. Sometimes he would forget that he had called, and a driver could stand there for an hour. I made it a point never to wait more than 15 minutes. Then I'd go back to the drivers' room and call to remind the staff man that I existed.)

When a staff member did appear at the window, he'd look over the surrounding area for spies. Workers for the cement company cater-corner across Romaine weren't considered spies. If there were no spies, the staff man would transmit his instructions. This was done by hollering. He'd holler down his assignment, and the driver would holler back to tell him that it was understood or to ask for clarification.

But the real touch of class came if there was to be any exchange of materials. Papers, books, envelopes, letters, bags, or any other small package would be relayed by the famous Operations fishline. They had a very short piece of fishing rod upstairs—perhaps three feet overall—that had a fishing reel attached. The fishline was nylon, probably 20-pound test. Tied to the end of the line was a clothespin. If the man in Operations had anything to be sent down to street level, he'd stick it into the jaws of the clothespin and let out enough line to allow the item to reach the outstretched hands of the driver. When something was being sent up, the procedure would be reversed, the item would be reeled up to the level of the window, and then a deft flick of the wrist would transfer it into the safety of Operations.

I received hundreds of items from Operations by way of the fishline. I was also hit on the head by quite a few books and heavy packages that had been improperly secured by the man at the window. The greatest problem, of course, was wind, especially when the item being transferred was money. We dealt in cash, and when the wind was over 15 knots, the fishline, clothespin, and envelope didn't have enough combined weight to keep the money from being tossed around, and often blown right off the line. I once chased an envelope almost to La Brea Avenue, one block west. (Wind stank, and so did rain: we'd always get half-soaked before we could get back into the car.)

The worst thing of all was having someone drive by as you were standing out there. Inevitably they would stare at you (especially if it was raining), and inevitably that would cause the cupcake up in Operations to pull a turtle and disappear from sight, and inevitably that would make at least one driver—me—feel like a 24-karat jerk. I would ache to shout at people driving by, "This may look stupid to you, me standing here playing with a fishline, but I am handling the personal communications of Howard Hughes, so you better believe it's important." I never did that, of course.

In addition to Operations, the second story also housed four or five other men who worked out of Howard Lundeen's office. Lundeen was responsible for, among other things, the H. L. Company, which handled property for Hughes. Hughes was forever leasing homes. He would always have some of our people looking for homes, leasing homes, guarding homes, or repairing the homes that had been under lease but had since been returned to their owners. (Later, when I began to spend a lot of time with Hughes, I found that the reason for this activity was Mrs. Hughes. Jean Peters was constantly pressuring Hughes to allow them to move out of the Beverly Hills Hotel and into a house. As long as Hughes had two or three houses under lease he could say that he was trying to comply with her wishes. Something, naturally, would always prevent his moving into one of these houses.)

The houses that Hughes leased were not tract homes. They were all in the $300,000–$1,000,000 price range, located in the most fashionable sections of L.A.—the more remote reaches of Beverly Hills, Holmby Hills, or Bel-Air. Whenever a new house was leased, it was put under a 24-hour-a-day guard. Nobody would be allowed to enter the grounds. Gardeners would be kept out, pool-maintenance men would be kept out, domestic help would be kept out. Do I need to say what the result would be? A well-maintained estate turns into a messy jungle in a very short time without the attention paid it by the people who work on it. The pool turns black with algae, landscaping overruns the flower beds, the lawns die; things go to hell in a hurry.

The road to hell was often paved by the guard detail. A well-known writer's Coldwater Canyon house, furnished with exquisite examples of Oriental art, was leased. As with all the other houses, once it was leased the owner, as well as everyone else whose responsibility it was to take care of the house, was kept away by the guards. A few months after the house had been taken over by Operations, I decided to take a turn on guard duty. The house had been stripped of all its artworks, and I knew they hadn't been put in storage because of the reaction of the owner and Bishop Lundeen when the owner came back to inspect the property before the end of the lease. I thought he was going to blow his cork. He was squeaking with rage, and Lundeen was crimson with embarrassment. Naturally, Hughes paid for what was missing. Hughes always paid. It would probably have made some sense if Hughes had ever gone to examine the places he leased, but that wasn't the case. He never went near them.

He never went near his secretary, either. The northeast offices upstairs on Romaine were taken over by secretaries, the head secretary being Nadine Henley, who was the long-time personal secretary to Hughes. She also used drivers, lowered things out of *her* window, and seemed to keep herself busy, although none of us knew with what.

*   *   *

I was at home when I got a call from Kay Glenn. It seemed, he said, that Bond would be on detached duty for some time (scuttlebutt would have it that he was on a supersecret, hush-hush assignment). Kay instructed me to take over full responsibility for running the drivers' room. I had worked for Hughes Productions for less than a year and now I was a responsible part of the management team, even though my pay remained at $2.00 an hour. There seemed to be no stopping the kid from Colorado. (Especially since I would get to approve my own time card, which could be construed as a raise.) During the months I had worked as a driver I had made mental notes of many, many changes that could be made to improve the economics of that arm of Hughes Productions. Although I had been as quick as anyone to take advantage of there never being questions asked about expense chits (in retrospect I figure that it was cheaper for them to allow us to pad our expenses than to pay us higher salaries and the concomitant higher state costs for Social Security, unemployment, and the like), now that I was on the other side I felt a responsibility to stop people from doing what I had been doing.

What I had mostly been doing was getting a lot of overtime, and I had been getting it because the scheduling was slapdash. So I worked my butt off devising a schedule for the 26 drivers that would eliminate the disparities that had one man working a 20-hour weekly schedule, while others would make up for it with overtime. I sent the schedule upstairs, noting that it would practically eliminate the overtime and save the company a lot of money. It was sent back with a terse marking: "Unworkable." I immediately called upstairs to find out *why*. The voice on the other end informed me "Joe B. can't work Thursday night. He has to be at a Mutual Meeting. Wayne L. can't work Monday because he has a Deacon's Meeting," and on and on. This was the first time I was told outright that the Mormon Church was more important to Operations than Hughes Productions. (I doubt that Howard Hughes knows that to this day.) Of course, I revised the schedule after conferring with the drivers to find out what their church responsibilities were, sent it upstairs, and got it immediately okayed.

Being a tiny bit vindictive, I decided to retaliate for what I viewed as a putdown. In addition to the normal drivers' duties, we were maintaining guard details at the airport, two houses, Mrs. Hughes's bungalow at the Beverly Hills Hotel, and an off-and-on detail at the home of one of the lawyers who represented Hughes. Most of the stations were manned on a 24-hour basis, but some were from sundown to sunup. I *knew* from my airplane-watching days that these assignments were handled casually, and so I began to check on the guard posts. All of them were being run the way the airport was when I had worked there. I chewed more asses in two weeks than the entire coyote population of the Southwest had in three years, and it really shaped up the troops. A few guys quit, but replacements came easily. Operations, of course, took no note of my zealous dedication.

Or did they? I was at home when I got a call from Harry James, a member of Operations. I was to report to the Goldwyn Studios on Santa Monica Boulevard that night at 7:00 P.M. My friend Bill Brimley would be at the guardhouse on Formosa Avenue and would give me further instructions. From the tremor in James's voice I knew this was something very big. But I was unprepared for what Brimley told me as we walked from the gate to a building on the south side of the studio.

"Ron, the Old Man is going to be screening some films here. We're supposed to guard him."

Chapter 7

It was a pleasant enough evening, but I suddenly felt quite chilly. I tried to remember anything in my employment interview in the gas station or anything I had said since then that would have caused someone to think I should or could serve as a bodyguard. I might have been a bit feistier than the Mormon kids working for Hughes, but I always figured that part of that was because I was a bit older, had served in the war, and hadn't just arrived in L.A. from Fleabite, Utah. But simply being feisty didn't, in my estimation, make for a bodyguard. Brimley lacked an inch on my 5′9″, but had 20 pounds on my 180; neither of us was calculated to inspire terror in the hearts of would-be attackers of the likes of Howard Hughes.

When we got to the building we made a quick tour. Our primary area of concern was the second floor, where the screening room was located. There was a hallway running the full length of the building—perhaps 150 feet long. At each end of the hall was a single door leading to the stairs coming up, which were outside the building, a tribute to the weather of southern California. That seemed to make it easy for us: two doors, two guards.

The building was a long rectangle, running from north

to south. On the west side of the second floor, all along the hallway, was a series of small rooms that served as offices and film-cutting rooms. They were all empty at that time of night. On the east side was a large screening room, perhaps 25 feet wide, and 100 feet long. It had theater chairs in the back half of the room. At the very back were two long, overstuffed benches that ran the width of the room. Behind them was the projection booth, which could only be reached by walking outside the room, down the hall to the south entrance, outside to the catwalk, and then along the catwalk to the one door to the projection booth, on the east side of the building at the southeast corner. The projection booth was telephonically connected with the screening room by a direct line that ran to a phone on a solid table in the middle of the theater. (There was another phone on the table that connected to the outside world through the Goldwyn switchboard, and a similar instrument in the projection booth.) It was a simple enough layout, and a cinch to cover.

Bill and I started to discuss our duties. I waited for him to give me instructions, and it became obvious that he was waiting for me, the head of the drivers' room, to give *him* some information. We both admitted that it was our first time on the job. Bill confessed that the only reason he knew what we were supposed to do was that he had kept his ears open and had overheard other drivers talking about the guard detail at Goldwyn.

So we went into the projection booth and called Operations for instructions. They were rattled off to us, no doubt from a sheet, by a staff member. It was the same old stuff about not looking at Hughes or speaking to him or touching him (unless, of course, he commanded us to do any of these things). We were also not to allow anyone up the stairways at the two ends of the building, were not ourselves allowed into the projection booth, and were not to smoke or drink on duty. The list went on and on, with an attention to minute detail that only a watchmaker could have enjoyed. We acknowledged that we understood it all (although I suspect that both of us were only admitting that we had *heard* it all).

Five minutes later we broke our first rule. A station wagon drove up to the stairway at the south end of the building. Three men got out of the car, put on white gloves, and began to carry a large white leather chair up the stairs. We recognized these guys as Hughes personnel. They had appeared on occasion at the drivers' room, but neither Bill nor I knew what it was they did. Our orders had been to allow no one up those stairs, but we figured that Operations had blown it again: it would be nuts not to allow these guys to hoist that chair up. We stepped aside and the men took the chair into the theater and placed it in the open front section. They quickly walked back downstairs and reappeared bearing an even larger white leather chair and an ottoman. The second chair and the ottoman were placed alongside the first chair in a manner so careful and exacting that you might have thought these guys were in training to build machines for the space program. (We saw this procedure repeated many times over the next months, and I swear the alignment of those damned chairs never varied by as much as one-sixteenth of an inch.) Without a word the three men left, leaving Bill and I to guard the chairs and ottoman and the empty studio.

Half an hour later we had another chance to display our authority. A man started up the south stairway and seemed to display every intention of coming right up. (That is, he didn't stand down at the bottom and ask us

68

if he *could* come up; he just started climbing.)

"Hold it right there, fellow," said Bill. I was impressed, but the man kept right on coming, which was no way to treat two rookie bodyguards.

"Fella, you'd damned well better stop right there," I said, as much to my surprise as anyone's. My powerful voice, ahem, seemed to have turned the trick: The man stopped. He stood on the staircase, looked straight at us, and wiped us out with two sentences.

"I'm Carl, the projectionist. Do you really want me to stand here or can I go into *my* booth and set up *my* equipment?" He had one hell of a point. We stepped aside and watched him walk around the corner to go into *his* projection booth. In less than half an hour we had trampled on Operations' instructions.

Bill and I stood on the outside-stairway landing and talked. He had a greater stock of funny stories than anyone I had ever met, and I was enjoying myself thoroughly when he suddenly said, "See you, pal," and took off on a dead run for the north side of the building. I looked down and saw a familiar blue Chevy heading for *my* stairway. (Bill was no dummy.) I threw a quick peek at Bill, down at the other end of the building, and was very impressed to see that he had assumed a rigid parade-rest position, standing in his doorway with his back to the corridor. From where I stood he looked ready to hold off a battalion of Hughes-haters.

I had a problem, though. I couldn't stand in *my* doorway because that would block the way of the approaching party. I couldn't move toward the projection booth because that would cause me to look toward the car and its occupants. I turned my back to the staircase, which ran along the east-west side of the building, and jammed my body against the outside railing that paralleled the open door. I was facing west and praying that I would not protrude so far into the path of the people coming in that my body might touch them. I heard footsteps on the staircase and as they reached my position, I heard them pass by me and go down the hall. I took a deep breath. I'd lucked out again. Howard Hughes and whoever was with him had been able to get inside without stumbling over Ron Kistler.

We fractured the next rule a couple of hours later. I heard voices from the opposite end of the hallway. I turned around and was astonished to see a studio watchman walking right down the middle of the hall. Directly opposite the main doorway to the theater he stopped, inserted a key into a time clock, twisted it, replaced the key in the key box, and walked slowly in my direction. "Evenin', son," he said as he walked down the stairs. Bill had followed him down the corridor and now joined me at my post.

"Ron," he said, "it looks like we are between the rock and the hard place. We've got rules, Operations has got rules, Hughes has probably got his own rules, Goldwyn has rules, and a lot of other damned fools have their rules. I figure that the best thing we can do is break some, bend some, ignore some, and enforce some so that the world will keep turning at its own pace." (This was the best set of instructions I was ever to hear while working for Hughes Productions. Nothing Operations ever said approached this for logic and sense.) I agreed with Bill that we would do our best without making too many waves.

Bill went back to his post, and I stayed at mine, listening to the muffled noises of the movie being shown inside. Suddenly the sound stopped, and I heard a loud *bang!* that sounded like a shot. I whirled toward the studio in terror, thinking that someone had gotten in somehow and had shot Howard Hughes. As I started toward the theater door, it exploded open and Hughes came out and started walking toward me. I stood, frozen, looking right at him. I knew that was the wrong thing, so I quickly turned and walked outside onto the catwalk toward the projection booth. I walked a few feet and stopped. Leaning against the railing and waiting for my pulse to slow down I didn't have time to be grateful that my first time guarding Hughes hadn't ended in disaster. The footsteps in the hallway were getting closer and closer. It became obvious that Hughes was about to come out on the catwalk where I was standing. If he was heading for the projection room I was sunk, for I wouldn't have any place to retreat to. While I was counting my nonexistent options I heard another *bang,* and I turned to see an outside door closing. I had been in the doorway for two hours and hadn't noticed that there was a restroom, marked *Women,* with a doorway on the landing. It was within three feet of where I'd been standing. Some bodyguard.

I heard the unmistakable sound of a tall man urinating into a bippy and *I* felt relieved. Now I knew *where* Howard Hughes was, *what* he was doing, and that he certainly would be coming out. I took a position about three feet from the door and turned my back. A short time later I heard the door open. There was a footstep, then another, then silence. The skin on the back of my neck began to crawl.

"Good evening, Ron." It was a man's voice, pleasant, well-modulated, and with just a trace of Texas twang. "You can turn around. Hell, I'm not *that* ugly." He chuckled. I turned around to face one of the world's greatest mysteries. There really *was* a Howard Hughes, even close up.

I looked up at a thin, angular face that was neatly framed by a Vandyke beard. He had thin gray hair that was combed straight back in a style that had gone out of fashion; there were traces of the original brown in his hair. He was over 6'3" and appeared to weigh no more than 155 pounds. He was dressed in a loose-fitting sport coat, a white shirt that was open at the neck, tan gabardine slacks that were not only out of style but seemed to have been tailored for a heavier man, and a pair of brown, wing-tip brogans. There were no laces in the shoes, and judging from the decrepit condition of the footwear, it looked as if the laces had died a natural death. It seemed to be the same outfit that Hughes had been wearing at the airport when I had first seen him.

How did he know my name? Perhaps he had asked about me after the incident at the airport. (How else could my advancement in the organization be explained?) I don't remember if I said hello back to him. As we stood there, leaning on the outside railing in the soft, California night, we exchanged small talk—very small. Hughes volunteered that it had been a nice day, and I replied, "Yes, but it was warm."

"The clouds are building," he said, "so it looks as if we'll have some more rain."

He didn't ask me how I was feeling, or anything about my personal life (married? children?), or anything else that two strangers might discuss to pass the time. Nor did he want to talk about my job, which is a subject that might be expected to be covered when the two strangers meeting are employer and employee.

Abruptly he went into a discourse, in great detail,

about the workings of a large tank used for storing natural gas that dominated the skyline next to the studio. I learned that the vaporous gas was held under a pressure of six psi, that the volume of gas would cause the top of the container to rise and fall proportionately to the contents, that it was easy to measure the contents by an outside scale, that the gas had been treated so that it would smell, and a great deal of other information that would drive a budding meter-reader crazy with ecstasy. We talked—rather he talked and I mostly listened— about the tank *for almost 45 minutes* before he returned to the screening room. A short time later the screening ended. As Hughes walked down the stairway to his car I waited for a "Goodnight, Ron." It never came. As the footsteps reached the bottom of the stairs I snuck a peek to see who Hughes had come with. All I could see were the back of a beautiful, full-length mink coat, the legs of a pair of blue slacks, and a pair of white canvas deck shoes. Bill strolled down to join me. He remarked that it was nice to see "the Major" again. That was what some of us called Jean Peters.

A short time later the chair detail arrived and removed the three pieces of furniture. The projectionist, Carl, left. So did we.

Chapter 8

The screenings continued for four months. For the first few weeks it meant a gorgeous amount of overtime, as Bill and I were tending to our normal duties during the day and then going over to Goldwyn at night. Virgie wasn't crazy about the fact that I was spending as many as five nights a week away from home, but it was a lot better (or perhaps a little better) for her that I was loafing around a movie studio than that I was squiring would-be movie stars to posh restaurants.

Every night was like the first one. First Bill and I would arrive, then the chairs, then Carl, and finally the guests of honor. The reverse procedure would take place to close things down. Bill and I were not to leave until the chairs had been safely loaded aboard the station wagon.

About three weeks after the screenings started, there was a break in the pattern. Everything followed form until Hughes and the Major left. When the chair detail left, they took with them only one of the chairs, the smaller one. Brimley and I just stood there, looking at each other. Since Carl hadn't left, we didn't either, and in about 30 minutes, perhaps 40, the Chevy reappeared. Hughes came back to continue his movie-watching—

alone. He kept it going until early the next morning.

Bill and I dragged ourselves back to the drivers' room and I called Virgie to tell her where I'd been, what I'd been doing, and to explain that I was going to crash on the couch in the dayroom for a couple of hours. It wasn't to be the last time, as Hughes began to stretch his screening schedules with alarming frequency. Soon he was coming without the Major.

Those solo sessions lasted from 48 to 72 hours. To prepare for the marathons we had to assemble a hell of a lot of film for Carl to show, so that Hughes could have a choice of movies. We knew that Hughes was coming alone when we found ourselves going all over the city (and sending other drivers, as well) to pick up film. Our sources were the libraries of the studios, producers' homes, film-rental companies, directors' homes, as well as the Hughes library at Operations.

Because there was an I'll-scratch-your-back-you-scratch-mine arrangement between the studios, and because Hughes was still considered to be in the movie business, we didn't have to pay for the films we got from the other studios. But we trampled all over the *spirit* of reciprocity, because it was impossible to predict just when Hughes would get around to signaling Carl to show a particular film.

To salve the people in charge of the film libraries at the studios, we made Christmas deliveries of booze and envelopes. I accidentally found out what was in those envelopes when Dick Homer and I were delivering some booze and an envelope to a guy at one of the major studios. I had been instructed to hand him the envelope, but we saw him walking at the studio gate and I gave Homer the envelope, which he slipped into the paper bag containing the gift-wrapped bottle. Homer leaned out of the car and handed the package to the executive, and we drove away. That night I got a frantic phone call from Operations. Had I delivered the envelope to Mr. So-and-So? Well, yes. But he says he didn't get it. I explained how the transfer had been made and the staff man was triumphant in his prissiness: Hadn't I been *told* to deliver the envelope personally? Hadn't I disobeyed instructions? Suddenly a thought—a hope—seized me and I hung up abruptly, dashed out of my house, and drove to the studio where the envelope had disappeared.

I went to the guard's office near the gate where we had seen the executive and explained that I had mislaid a paper bag that afternoon and could I look in his wastebasket? I described the envelope before diving into a trash bin that mercifully seemed not to have been emptied that day. Sure enough, there was a crumpled-up paper bag and in it a crumpled-up envelope. I got the address of the studio executive and drove over with the envelope, which he opened in front of me . . . just to be certain that everything was on the up-and-up. (He had turned around with the booze and given it to the guard on the gate, and the guard had taken the bottle and thrown out the bag without looking in it.) The envelope contained five crisp $100 bills. That was obviously Operations' way of saying thank you for bending some rules about the borrowing of films for Mr. Hughes's use.

Hughes would use the films he saw in these marathon sessions in strange ways. (His tastes ran from then-current Academy Award contenders to epics such as *I Was a Teenage Werewolf.*) He'd watch some of the films from beginning to end. Others he would signal to be stopped after 5, 10, 40, or 80 minutes. To this day I cannot figure out why he stopped some films when he did: On many occasions he would watch a movie for two hours and stop it five minutes from the end.

You really had to be an *avid* moviegoer to sit in a damned screening room for two, three, or four days at a time, and, the comfort of that leather chair notwithstanding, you certainly had to have a cast-iron ass. Bill and I had worked out a program that allowed us an occasional nap, but it was really hard on the projectionist, Carl. He had no relief, except for some Early Times bourbon that mysteriously found its way into the projection booth whenever a marathon screening was in the works. During the first day Hughes would bedevil Carl by making hand signals indicating that the picture was just a fraction out of focus. It was obvious that Hughes was just testing Carl to make certain he was awake, and it would infuriate Carl no end. In the privacy of the booth he would mutter that the old fart should get some glasses and would retaliate against Hughes by throwing the picture so far out of focus that you couldn't even glance at the screen without your eyes going buggo. He'd then focus it, but so slowly and carefully that it took an interminable length of time for the picture to be returned to the level of sharpness it had had when Hughes started his little game.

As you can tell, Bill and I had started spending a lot of time in the projection booth. While Carl never exactly invited us in, neither did he throw us out, so we felt as if we belonged. (One of the things we really belonged to was the warmth hidden in those bottles of Early Times.) Our rationalization was that we could look out of the window of the booth and see Hughes. Any time Hughes signaled for the film to stop—he'd wave his arms over his head in a crisscross motion—Bill and I would break for our stations. After Carl had ascertained that Hughes wanted to leave the theater and had turned on the lights, Hughes would make his way to the door and, by the time he got to the hallway, he would always find us—if he really noticed—alertly guarding his domain.

Aside from the Early Times and the naps, we would sustain ourselves with food. Carl followed the book by calling Operations, which would then transmit his order, often incorrectly, to the drivers' room. Bill and I cut out the middlemen, and quite often I would—as head of the drivers' room—assign a driver to sleep on the couch and be ready to bring us our orders of food. The only time Bill or I really violated orders was when we'd leave the premises to get something to eat or to take a quick piss. (We never used the toilet upstairs, for reasons I'll get to in a minute.)

Our forays for food were rather minor: During normal working hours one or the other of us would on occasion run down to the cafeteria on the lot and grab a carton or two of coffee to go and perhaps a piece of pie. Then we'd hustle back up to our posts. The only time either of us would leave to eat was when Hughes would drive the Major back to their hotel, the Beverly Hills, and the chair detail would leave his chair, indicating that he'd be back. I'd race up to Tiny Naylor's at the corner of Sunset and La Brea and grab a bite and race back to the studio. Then Bill would haul up there and get some food. We found that we both could make it in the 30 to 45 minutes it took Hughes to get the Major home and return to Goldwyn. Only one person didn't eat when Hughes was at Goldwyn: Hughes.

Obviously, the greatest problem during the extended sessions lay in the fact that the only part of the building that was being rented out to Hughes Productions was the screening room and the projection booth. The rest of the building was on a business-as-usual basis, which meant that film cutters, sound technicians, and office help reported to their assigned spaces on the west side of the second floor every working morning. To get to their offices they had to walk up the stairways we had been ordered not to have them walk up, and they had to walk down the hallway that they certainly were not supposed to be walking down.

Hell, those people had to make a living, and so Bill and I bent, broke, and ignored the rules that Operations had sworn us to uphold. When one of the people who worked in those offices approached the area for the first time, we headed him off and delivered a little speech.

"We know that you have to get into your office to work. You certainly have the right to do that. However, we have a little problem. We work for Mr. Howard Hughes, and he is viewing movies in the projection studio at this very moment. He has asked us not to allow anyone into that part of the building. We'd like to do what he says and still make you happy, so can we make a deal?"

It is a tribute to the good nature of ordinary people that everyone who worked there made that deal with us. The deal was that when they wanted to go to their offices they would signal us. If Hughes was in the projection room, intent on his film, we would hurry them into their offices. They had to agree to keep their doors closed at all times so that Hughes wouldn't be able to see them. When they wanted to leave they would signal us and wait for us to give them the all-clear. On getting that signal, they would hustle out of the building. If Hughes was in the john, or headed that way, we would keep everyone out of sight until he got back into the studio. His use of that john, though, gave us some trouble. I mentioned that Bill and I never used the toilet up there. The reason was that you could only say that the toilet area was in piss-poor shape after Hughes got through with it. His aim was, to put it charitably, casual—so casual, in fact, that Bill and I had to field some complaints from a nice female film cutter who worked upstairs and who didn't mind the cloak-and-daggers we put her through to get into and out of her work area. But she did object mightily to being faced with the choice of a massive mop-up job or a run for a faraway toilet whenever nature called her.

Had she ever been able to complain directly to Hughes, he might have told her that running is good exercise. I was to learn of his interest in physical exercise while at Goldwyn. We had been there, on that occasion, for two and a half days, and it looked as if the Old Man was never going to leave. Bill, Carl, and I were exhausted, and only our supply of Early Times made us think that we could outlast the pain and strain of being there. The three of us were in a state of euphoria that the W.C.T.U. would probably describe as being drunk. We were still functioning, though. Bill and I would take turns in the projection booth so that Carl could grab a ten-minute snooze during a reel. (Whenever the signals would appear on the film to start up the second projector we'd nudge Carl awake, he'd start it going, then rewind off the first projector, set up a new reel, and nod out again.)

It was the middle of the night, and Hughes was watching some movie so awful that it had driven me out of the booth and up to the north end of the corridor. I was leaning back in a chair with my legs propped against the opposite side of the doorway. It was my superguard position. Someone would have to brush my legs aside or step over them in order to get into the hallway.

I was dozing when I heard a terrible noise—footsteps, many of them, coming down the hallway. My first drowsy, terrified thought was that the murderers were running down the corridor and into the studio and good-bye Howard Hughes, and good-bye Ron Kistler's job. I got upright somehow, focused on the hall, and saw that there was only one person running down the hall, and that person was Howard Hughes. He was headed for the other end of the corridor, and I figured, oh, boy! He's run out the door and the murderers are still in there. They haven't got him yet. When Hughes got about ten feet from the doorway at the south end he planted both feet, threw his weight back on his heels, and slid—all the way to the doorway. In my boozy state, I decided that he had seen one of the murderers on the landing and had taken evasive action. But I couldn't, for the life of me, figure out what was taking the rest of the murderers so long to get out of the studio . . . unless, of course, they had turned their savage attention on those poor guys in the projection booth.

Suddenly I heard the thunder of more footsteps. I looked down the hall and there was Hughes, running full speed toward me. His knee action was good considering that his spindly legs were way too long for the rest of him; his arm and hand movements were worthy of Roger Bannister in his prime. He was *really* making tracks, and by then it was dawning on me that there was no one after him. Whatever Hughes was doing, he was doing because he wanted to. As he got closer I got my chair and myself out of the way, and when he was ten feet from me he planted both heels again and slid—whooie! did he slide! The north end of the hallway got much less traffic than the other end, so the floor wax hadn't been worn down.

He was gaining speed when he hit the doorway, and the slight elevation of the doorframe caused him to go airborne—like a skier coming off a mogul—and he literally *flew* into the pipe railing of the outside staircase. I thought he was sure to pitch over, fall to the ground, and break his neck. Terrific. How the hell would I explain *that* to Operations?

He slowly unwrapped his lanky frame from the railing and looked at me with a sheepish grin. Without a word he turned back into the hallway and started running. When he got to that predetermined spot at the other end, he went into another virtuoso slide. He made a U-turn and headed back my way. I made damned certain that I was well out of the action zone. But Hughes is a fast study, so there was no way he would overshoot this time. He started his slide about five feet farther back and came to a halt with his toes barely touching the doorframe. He made about ten round trips that night (and many more on subsequent nights).

When he had completed his runs and walked back into the studio and the sound of a movie filtered out into the hall, I ran down to the other end and found Bill. "For Christ's sake, Bill—did you *see* that?" Bill looked at me and said simply, "I saw." Later we figured that Hughes did this to wake himself up and get the circulation going in his legs, after hours and days of sitting in that same chair.

But after that display of athletic prowess I made a resolution about my guarding of Hughes: If someone *did* come after him to do him harm, I'd simply stand out of the way and yell, "Run, Mr. Hughes! Run!" Hell, I figured he could outrun 99 percent of his would-be attackers; the other 1 percent he could simply slide around.

During our third month at Goldwyn, Hughes began spending more and more time alone in marathon sessions. He would always bring Kleenex boxes with him, even when he was with the Major. Now he was bringing in a couple at a time and starting to stack and restack them. He was using the Kleenex to clean everything within reach—the chair, his fingernails, his ears. It seemed from the projection booth that this was more a nervous habit than anything else: he didn't seem to be concentrating on the fact that he was *cleaning* something; it seemed to be an outlet for nervous energy. Scuttlebutt had it that business matters were pressing down on him: TWA was having major problems. My thought was that the more business pressure there was on Hughes, the more he would turn to the movies. I suspect that Hughes did his best mental work—at that time, anyway—watching movies, since he wasn't the kind of guy to sit at a desk and make lists.

As if his schedule weren't difficult enough for Carl, Hughes, during the last two months in the studio, took to stopping a film and motioning Carl to come down out of the projection booth and into the theater. Carl would make the long trip, and Hughes would give him instructions to rerun a part of the film that had been shown earlier. (Hughes preferred not to have to get out of his chair and walk the ten feet to the phone where he could speak to Carl without having the projectionist walk 100 yards or so, round trip. But what's money for, anyway, if not comfort?)

Some of these segments would be shown five or ten times before Hughes would allow Carl to continue with the rest of the film. It took me a few times to figure out what was really going on during those reruns. There was always a particular item of interest on the screen and, generally speaking, that item was a female member of the cast. She might be sitting in the rear of a crowd, one of the extras who serve to create atmosphere on a street or in a club, but no matter how minuscule her part she was the target of Howard Hughes's undivided attention. After making certain that the identification of the girl was properly noted by Carl (with hand signals this time), the film would be continued. Carl would write down the data necessary and call Operations with it: the name of the movie, the reel number, how far into the reel, the scene, and a description of the woman. Operations would track down the casting director for that film and he or she would run down the name.

This information would be sent to Walter Kane, the head talent agent for Hughes Productions. Kane would contact the actress or her agent (if she had one). Some of these women would be given contracts that would allow them to be driven around in Chevys by nice young Mormon men who worried about jiggling their breasts while going over the railroad tracks on Santa Monica Boulevard. The other side of the coin was that we often screened older films at Goldwyn, and one time Hughes signaled his interest in a woman who was finally tracked down, weeks and weeks later, in Florida, where she was a happy grandmother—not quite what Hughes had in mind.

The screenings had become so commonplace that it looked as if we might be at Goldwyn forever. It was okay with me, since my overtime more than made up for my physical discomfort. Besides, there were always a few days off between marathons when I could go home and convince Virgie that she was, too, more important than Howard Hughes.

Things changed very quickly. "Our" screening room

was used to show rushes of *Porgy and Bess,* which was then being shot at Goldwyn, to the cast. Although I had never heard Hughes express any bigotry or racism, the fact that an all-black cast had been in that theater affected him or someone in Operations to the extent that Hughes never went back into that room. The Goldwyn days were over for Howard Hughes, and over for Ron Kistler.

It was a hell of a letdown to be back in the drivers' room after being with the Old Man. Doing little errands for Operations was pale stuff after having been with Hughes and having been invested with his power in dealing with Operations.

The authority we used on the outside, after all, came in the form of cash. We were laying it on a lot of people to get things done. For example, we'd get a call from Operations that that special starlet (we called her "the Party") would be going to Grauman's Chinese Theater on a certain night and she'd be driving herself in her expensive convertible. Operations would order us to make certain that she could park her car on the street near the theater.

Well, there're a hell of a lot of ways you can get your head beat in trying to save a parking space on a busy street, so what I did (and the other drivers with sense did) was to go to Hollywood Boulevard hours and hours before the Party was supposed to arrive and plant one of our cars there. It would get a ticket, of course, for violating a parking regulation, but so what? I'd be in that car when the Party arrived, and when I saw her blue Imperial come around the corner I'd pull out and let her have the parking space. Other times I'd see a guy parking his car where I wanted her to park and I'd ask him, how long are you going to be? Then I'd give him $10 to leave when I wanted him to leave.

Whenever we had to go to Palm Springs or some other place that required our spending more cash than usual, we'd have to see a guy who lived in the Hancock Park section of L.A. That area is fairly close to Hollywood and was *the* ritzy place for film stars to live in the twenties. There are a lot of big houses but, unlike other areas that are fashionable but then are not, Hancock Park is still loaded with people who have money; it's L.A.'s area for WASP power.

Anyway, if you had to get a $1,000 or $1,500, you'd go to this guy's house. I assume that he was called by Operations and told that Ron would be there and would require such-and-such an amount. The first time I went there I couldn't believe it. I knocked on the guy's door, and after we had said hello he asked me to follow him. We walked from the front porch onto his driveway and back to his garage, which was unlocked. He raised the garage door, took his car keys out, and opened the trunk of his big Buick. Inside the trunk was a valise, and inside the valise was what had to be $250,000 in cold cash. I had never seen anything like it: a whole suitcase full of money.

It was clean money, too. That was one of the fetishes of the organization. The money had to be very neat, very fresh, very new. From time to time I'd get sent on a replenishing errand by this Hancock Park banker. He'd give me a check and tell me to go over and see the vice-president at a local branch of the Bank of America. I'd give that guy the check and our laundry list of what we needed: say, one hundred $100 bills, a lot of $50s, $20s, $10s, and so on. Always minty fresh. Of course, the bank cooperated fully.

I always used to wonder what would happen if you wanted to make an unauthorized withdrawal from this guy's Buick. I figured that anyone who walked up that driveway without being cleared would have more cameras on him than Jackie Onassis, his footsteps would be recorded, and some gorilla would have his ass within about three steps.

Playing with that money was the exciting work. The dreadful stuff was not only the ordinary errands for Operations, but having to feed them. The staff people could not leave the building, so it was necessary to bring their meals in. Most major cities have coffee shops near, or in, most office buildings. Not L.A. The nearest food was a burger stand a half-block away, across from the concrete company. That wasn't what Operations was about to eat, so an elaborate ritual took place.

The driver had to find out how many people were eating and then get them to agree on a common restaurant (the newer, dumber drivers might wind up going to four or five restaurants). The driver would go to the eatery and get the menu. Then he'd go to a phone and call Operations. He'd read the menu to one of the staff (sometimes having to read it to each staff member separately). The order was transmitted, and it was never simple. There were always variations: hold the pickle, no mayonnaise, lemon juice on the salad, tomatoes instead of potatoes, broccoli instead of soup—on and on until the damned thing was super a la carte. Then everything had to be boxed individually so that the staff people could find their orders.

The driver would haul the food back to 7000 Romaine and one of the staff would come down and carry everything upstairs (it would take three or four trips, but of course the driver could not help out). Then the driver would head around the corner and start making out his expense chit for the meal. Invariably the phone would ring three or four times with complaints from a staff member about a screwed-up order, cold food, or something else gone wrong. The whole process would take two hours to wrap up, and it was never to the satisfaction of Operations. For that matter, the restaurant people got to the point where they hated to see us walk in; even overlarge tips wouldn't placate them.

Operations came up with another self-feeding scheme that was truly amazing. They decided to have their meals catered by the cooks in the cafeteria at Hughes Aircraft near Playa del Ray, a mere *ten miles away* from Romaine Street in Hollywood. The specific instructions to the drivers were to drive carefully, so that the various sauces and gravies didn't mix with each other. I took that ride to be another wonderful opportunity to explore the laws of physics as they related to automotive design: How much could a Chevy take in the way of g forces when it was cornered hard? The sound of sauces slopping was music to my ears.

But the most unpleasant thing about being off the Goldwyn detail was the fact that one of the Operations staff, a young man who had previously given me some damned lucrative assignments, suddenly decided to take me into his confidence. He was working the graveyard shift, which meant that he was alone up there, and there was usually only one driver available. One night he called me up to Operations and told me about his life—for two hours. He had been converted to Mormonism, which was just about the high point of his existence. I did my best to appear interested since this guy was my gift horse. But I had the queasy feeling that I had heard one shoe drop.

The other one fell one night when I was at home. It was this guy from Operations, asking me if I'd like to go to Acapulco. I thought it was a Hughes project, so I said sure, terrific, and then I wanted to know what Hughes had going down there. Of course, it wasn't a Hughes project. It was a little vacation that this guy and a friend of his were taking. How to say no gracefully? Well, money was tight. No problem, he said. They would pick up my tab. There was only one thing left to do—use Virgie (who had been snuggling close to overhear the proposition and had been cleverly muttering about how *well* I had fooled her). I told the guy that my wife wouldn't let me go, which placated him.

But it left me feeling even more sour about the job, so I began to think about finding some more conventional form of employment—something with a realistic schedule, a sense of accomplishment, a future, and a pay scale of more than $2.00 an hour. I was saved from this dire fate by the bell of my home phone. Kay Glenn called with another assignment that would take me away from the drivers' room.

Chapter 9

Kay told me to report that evening to an address on Sunset Boulevard. He also gave me some unusual instructions. I was to treat the assignment confidentially—so much so, in fact, that I was not even to tell my wife about it. I was to report to the address, keep all strangers out, and wait for further orders.

It figured that the assignment had to do with Hughes. I drove over the mountains and down to Sunset after dinner. The address was a small office complex on the west end of the Sunset Strip, about a mile and a half east of the Beverly Hills Hotel. I found a sign directing people looking for the specific address I'd been given to go around the building to a parking lot in back. It turned out to be Martin Nosseck's Projection Studio, occupying a small bunch of rooms in the basement of the building. As I drove into the lot, I noticed some activity in a set of rooms and balconies above the parking area. I soon learned that a famous pop composer maintained an apartment there. Inside Nosseck's, I found two experienced Hughes drivers, Norm Love and Lloyd Hurley. As we waited in a small lobby area off the back parking lot, we were joined by projectionist Carl. A few minutes later the white-glove detail arrived with the white leather chairs.

A few minutes after that Hughes and the Major arrived and went immediately into the theater. Within a short time we heard the sound of the picture being run. Looking around, I couldn't understand why there had to be three of us there when Brimley and I had been enough at Goldwyn. Nosseck's occupied a relatively small area compared with the Goldwyn building.

Walking in from the parking lot, you faced a small lobby, with a couch and a bar and a coffee table. Immediately inside the door, on the right, was a minuscule toilet area with a washstand and crapper (which was so close to the opposite wall that anyone six feet tall had to sit up *very* straight or risk wedging himself in). To the left as you entered was a small room used for editing films. It also contained the building's electrical board, a fact that later proved to be of more than a little interest to me. As you walked in there was a couch along the left wall and a Coke machine on the right wall. Another cutting room opened off the left wall, while there was a door on the right that led to the stairs up to the rest of the building and the main entrance off Sunset Boulevard. When you got to the back wall, you could either turn left and go up to the projection booth, turn right and go into Mr. Martin Nosseck's office, or go straight, through a very solid, heavy wood door into the theater.

Putting one guard at the door to the parking lot and one guard at the door to the stairs still left one man sitting around that small lobby on one of the couches or hiding in the projection room. Besides, both doors could be locked from our side, so we didn't have to worry about any intruders at all, except those who might throw themselves through locked doors to get at Hughes. The three of us sat on the small, comfortable sofa, exchanging gossip. From time to time I would wander up to the projection booth to join Carl and watch parts of the movies (that first screening was a double feature).

At the end of the second film Hughes and the Major appeared and left the building. Within moments the white-glove detail appeared, went into the theater, and retrieved the smaller chair. Okay, so the Old Man was going to come back and continue watching films. It had happened enough times that I was ready for it.

But after Hughes returned and took his place in the theater, he called the three of us into the room with him. We stood directly in front of his chair and, at Hughes's motion, assumed the at-ease position.

"Fellows," he said, "I'm pleased that you all are here. I asked for you personally since I *know* each of you personally and know that you are the only people I can trust for this type of assignment." Our collective chest swelled about six inches at that.

"We will be here for quite a spell," Hughes said, "so I'll leave it up to you to work out your schedules so that there is at least one alert, well-rested person here at all times." With a three-man detail this seemed to me to be a license to steal.

"Absolutely no one is to know that you are here," Hughes continued. Well, I could think of five people (the white-glove detail, Jean Peters, and Kay Glenn) in the Hughes organization or close to the Old Man who already knew we were there.

As if to immediately contradict himself, Hughes said, "You may designate one of the drivers whom you all know and trust to bring in food, deliver messages, and run any errands for you." (Well, that made *six* people. Plus Virgie made seven.) "I will give you your instructions individually, starting with Lloyd, so you other two fellows can go back into the lobby until I call for you." End of audience.

I ran for the projection booth, naturally, so that I could see, if not hear, the next scene. It was one of the smartest things I've ever done, since I was privy to a fantastic sight. Lloyd had apparently been instructed to take a seat in a chair that was slightly to the rear of the Old Man's position. This chair was of the dining-room variety—no arms, not much padding—and was up against a wall. As Lloyd sat there, Hughes began to arrange and rearrange six boxes of Kleenex on a small coffee table that was on the left side of his chair. From my vantage point I could tell that Hughes wasn't saying anything; neither was Lloyd. All that was happening was the geometric rearrangement of those boxes. Every so often Hughes would glance over his shoulder to make certain that Lloyd was still there. He was, even though he was obviously getting damned uncomfortable sitting on that chair.

After two hours Hughes turned to Lloyd and evidently told him he could leave. I beat it back to the lobby, and Lloyd told Norm to go inside. When Norm had, I asked Lloyd what the boss had told him. "Nothing," he said. I went back to the projection booth, to see the same scene being played. Hughes was stacking and Norm was sitting. I started to think what I would, or should, do when my turn came.

Two hours later Norm got up and went outside. I joined him, and he told me that the boss wanted me. I asked him if he had received any other messages. Not surprisingly, he hadn't.

I went into the theater. Hughes was sitting there, and he said, after I had closed the door, "Ron, take a seat in the chair over by the wall. Sit there quietly until I tell you to move." I had seen this movie, so I determined, as I went to the chair and sat down, that I simply would not allow myself to be used the way the other two guys had been. I watched Hughes playing with his Kleenex boxes for a while and then I carefully and quietly slid off the chair and walked to the rear of the room, where a long couch had been placed against the rear wall. I stood there, arms behind my back, intently looking at the ceiling.

Hughes's high-pitched voice rang through the room. "Ron! What are you doing there? I told you to sit in the chair and wait until I told you to move. What are you *doing?*"

It was now or never. I tried to sound confident. "I'm looking for flies."

"Have you *seen* any flies?" Hughes wanted to know.

"No, but it sure beats sitting in that damned chair."

It was a toss-up as to what would happen next. I expected a verbal barrage, but Hughes began to chuckle, then laugh. "You've caught on," he said. "You can go outside now."

I went out into the lobby, closing the door behind me, and I began laughing so hard that I couldn't explain to Norm or Lloyd why I had been in the room only 15 minutes when they had been in there two hours. (Judging from the rules that existed for our behavior around Hughes and the way he acted at the airport and at Goldwyn, I had figured that he liked to know just how far he could push people around: When he had been dealing with men he respected, such as the airplane-moving crew, he neither insisted that they observe all the Hughes-is-holy rules, nor did they volunteer to do so. But it takes some sense of self-assurance to stand up to your boss when he's being absolutely unreasonable or ornery, and it isn't often done, I suppose. It certainly wasn't done in the Hughes organization by the people in Operations.)

The three of us sat there in the lobby as the movies droned on inside. We were not calculating complicated schedules—after all, three men, twenty-four hours, is a simple equation. As *experienced* Hughes employees, we were simply following the 40-by-Tuesday routine that some of us had developed in order to make up for our staggeringly bad rate of pay. The idea was to try and get your 40 hours of straight time in by Tuesday, thereby making the rest of the workweek a bonanza of time and a half. (I justified this to myself and my friends as being personal initiative, as opposed to overtime dictated by the Mormon Church.) So we sat and gossiped the night away. (Since we were all reasonably young, there was also something to the idea of staying up because the Old Man was staying up.)

The next day we learned the effects of what I had done in the studio. Norm, Lloyd, and I were sitting in the lobby when we heard Hughes call for us. That is, he bellowed loud enough for us to hear through the thin wall of the theater. (He knew we were all there, since he had seen us on a trip to the head.) We went inside, and Hughes made an announcement.

"I want you all to reschedule yourselves," he said, "so that Ron is here at all times. Norm, you and Lloyd can split your schedule so that one of you is here when the other is gone." With that he dismissed us, and we went back to the lobby.

Some fast calculating showed that, with 40 hours straight time and a can't-be-beat *128* hours a week over-time, my pay would zoom to $464 a week. Hughes hadn't said anything about my sleeping accommodations (but then he hadn't been too interested where—or if—Brimley, Carl, or I slept at Goldwyn). Norm and Lloyd chose up to see who would stay on the first of their 12-on, 12-off schedule. Norm went home, and Lloyd and I settled down to our vigil.

The first couple of days went fairly quickly, with Hughes inside the theater and us outside, occasionally peeking out the door at the beautiful early summer weather. But there was something strange happening inside that theater. Hughes wasn't watching movies non-stop, as he had at Goldwyn. Instead, he was just sitting there, stacking and restacking Kleenex boxes.

That seemed to be something he could do at the hotel, and the first delivery of food to Hughes indicated to me that we wouldn't be staying at Nosseck's for very long. Johnnie Holmes, Hughes's personal driver, arrived after two days with a brown-paper grocery bag. (These kraft paper bags were ordered in large lots by Operations, and then, because the bags were considered "too hot"—that is, contaminated by human hands—would be allowed to sit for *two years,* after which their germs were thought to have disappeared. Those germs probably died of boredom, but after two years the bags were okay for use in carrying things to Howard Hughes.) Anyway, Holmes took the bag inside to Hughes. His approach to Hughes, as viewed from the projection booth, was almost ritualistic.

Holmes walked down the right side of the studio until he hit Hughes's line of vision. There he stopped, standing perfectly still until the Old Man signaled him to approach his chair. Holmes stood in front of the chair, and evidently on command he bent over, held the bag at waist-high level, and at a 45-degree angle with the opening facing Hughes. Hughes took three or four pieces of

Kleenex in his right hand, covering the palm, and very carefully lowered that hand into the bag. He was so careful not to touch the sides of the bag that you would have thought that the container's last use had been to haul samples of bubonic plague.

Hughes brought out an item from the bag and carefully placed it on the coffee table next to his chair. It was a quart of milk. He reached in again . . . slowly . . . and brought out a Hershey bar (with almonds). He put that on the table. Another reach into the bag, another Hershey bar was brought out. Another reach brought out the final item, a four-ounce package of pecan nuts. With that, Holmes folded up the then-empty bag and left the room.

I figured that Holmes had brought by a snack for Hughes, but when the Old Man ate the candy and nuts and drank the milk—taking a few *hours* to do so—I realized that what he got was all he was going to get.

Well, his incredible eating habits had been part of the drivers' room scuttlebutt among the older drivers, and even though I knew Hughes was capable of some pretty odd things in the culinary department (his fasts at Goldwyn, for example), I thought that soon enough either he'd get some real food or go to the hotel to eat.

Was I wrong! So there I sat, reading dog-eared copies of the Hollywood trade papers that lay around the lobby of Nosseck's. There was a time when I had practically memorized those copies of *Daily Variety, The Hollywood Reporter,* and *Billboard.* And still Hughes stayed inside that theater, stacking those boxes.

By the third day time had slowed to an imperceptible crawl. There was nothing of interest doing for us, and since Hughes wasn't watching movies, there wasn't even anything for us to look at. Then Hughes gave us a new responsibility. He said that he wanted us to open the theater door for him when he left the room or when he wanted to go back inside. That didn't sound like a major problem: if Hughes wanted the door to be opened, certainly two able-bodied men who were bored silly could open the door for him.

We reckoned without Hughes. The way he signaled that he wanted out was to kick hell out of the door. Apparently, no one had evaluated that door for its acoustical properties, which were considerable. When he kicked that damned door it sounded like someone shooting off a small cannon. The immediate effect of that on us poor guards was stark terror. The fellow closest to the door—slouched on the couch next to it—should have been the first person there, but the *boom!* of Hughes's kick invariably caused him to leap from the couch (and *away* from the door). There would be a rush for the door on the part of the second man (and, once he had pulled himself together, the first), but we were usually too late to satisfy Hughes. Which meant that we'd get the worst of the worst—a second kick. We knew it was coming, but there was no way for the nervous system to roll with that punch. This had a telling effect on Norm. After a few days he told us that he didn't want to put up with the strain, and left. He was replaced by Fred Jayka.

There was no way of adequately telling Fred what he was getting into, except that anyone who was at all sharp could have smelled a rat. Put another way, he certainly should have been able to smell Kistler and Hughes. I didn't know when I was going to get home, and I didn't know if Virgie would let me in when I got there. I had, after all, been sitting there for a week in the same clothes. So had Hughes, but Hughes had taken to quickly washing himself down in the basin of that tiny bathroom. Actually, that's overstating what he did. He was splashing himself with water. What he threw on his head trickled down and presumably cleaned what it touched. But what it touched in terms of area was limited by the absorbency of his skin and the clothes he wore: both tended to drink up the water before much of it could get down to where the real action was.

As I sat there smelling myself and the Old Man, I began to get more and more disenchanted with my job. When I had gone to Goldwyn and been thrown into direct contact with Hughes, I had felt that there was potential for me in the organization—if not with the Mormon honchos in Operations, at least with Hughes himself (and I knew where the money ultimately came from). The idiotic schedule we worked over there, the dumb things we did—all contributed in a strange way to the intrigue of the job. I began to enjoy the select, untouchable status that you get in the Hughes organization when you actually are with Hughes himself. It was my way of being able to tell the creeps in Operations to blow it out. Now I was at Nosseck's because Mr. Howard Hughes had personally asked that Ron Kistler be there. That's how I took it.

But the sanitation problem was going to be more than I could bear. I've always been a clean person. My body was accustomed to being bathed at least once a day. I detested body odor and stale breath. At Nosseck's I had both. And I felt that it would really upset Hughes if I mentioned my problem to him. After all, he was in the same state except for those puny little spritz-baths, and I was afraid he would ask that I follow his example.

Finally, after my clothes started talking to me, I decided I had to do something drastic. I waited until I thought Hughes would be trying to sleep and I went home. After about an hour and a half in the bathroom and a change into clean clothes, I began to feel human. Virgie tried to talk me into staying home with her and the children, but I felt compelled to go back. After all, Hughes *couldn't* stay in there much longer. But to hedge that bet I took a toilet kit and some clean slacks and sport shirts with me.

When I got back to Nosseck's I was pleased to learn that Hughes had done nothing in my absence except play with his Kleenex boxes. The test would come, I supposed, when Hughes saw me. I had on fresh clothes, had shaved, and had obviously violated his order that I *be there*. He looked me over quite closely during his next trip through the lobby but didn't say a word about it.

Hughes had another hygienic bombshell for us. In those first days we had all been sharing the john, which was no problem since the other two men had access to their toilets at home. Carl and the rest of us *had*, of course, been forced to confront Hughes's unconcern about aim. That was bad enough, but Hughes himself dealt with it (and the resulting possibility of germs) by wrapping everything in great wads of the cheap paper towels that were dispensed in the washroom. He had covered the room with them—seat, basin, floor.

Then he announced to us on leaving the john that the rest of us would have to find someplace else to relieve ourselves. Since we weren't supposed to leave the studio when we were on duty, this order presented us with a problem. It presented *me* with the biggest problem of all, because I theoretically was *never* to leave the studio. Using perfect logic, we decided that *I* was to be the biggest victim and so it was up to *me* to face down Howard Hughes.

The next time he came out of the john, I stood up and said, looking as solemn as possible, "I have to piss."

He looked at me as if I'd lost my marbles. But he didn't reply. So I tried again.

"I have to piss, and there is no place for me to piss since you won't allow us to use your crapper." Well, I figured, I had him.

Or did I? He walked around me and without a word went back into the theater. The door closed behind him. End of discussion. But about a half hour later I heard a bellow from inside.

"Ron! Come in here!"

I went inside and stood before him. He rolled his eyes, trying to look very bored.

"Ron, I'm sorry you have to piss." Well, at least that made two of us who were sorry. "I'm not going to let you fellows use the bathroom down here, so we will have to find a way for you to relieve yourselves." I like a man who can identify a problem and go to work on it.

"Ron, there are some ice buckets here, are there not?" He was not unobservant: Johnnie Holmes had brought some ice buckets over from the hotel to keep Hughes's milk cool in case the Old Man was asleep when Holmes arrived with the bag of food. They were really classy ice buckets, green and white, bearing the exalted inscription "Beverly Hills Hotel."

"Use the cutting room closest to the front door," Hughes said. "Keep the empty buckets in there and use them to piss in." He pointed to the door to the lobby and I left, certain that the fisheye I had just got from Hughes was because I hadn't been smart enough to think of such a simple solution to the problem.

But that solution was batty enough to make me queasy just thinking about it. You of course have thought of the great objection to the plan: What were we supposed to do when we had to move our bowels? If Hughes actually thought that we were going to squat over some damned plastic ice buckets, he was beyond description.

I told Lloyd and Fred and Carl about Hughes's plan and told the other drivers to try and schedule their bowel movements when they were at home. (Carl, who had had the foresight to have a cot delivered to the projection room, had taken to leaving during the long intervals when the Old Man wasn't waiting to see films. He, too, could use toilets elsewhere.) But we were still supposed to use those buckets when we had to take a leak.

Or, rather, my coworkers would have to use them. I had been sneaking upstairs to the other part of the office building to use the men's room up there. I had started using it when I found Hughes's aim to be so abysmal that he was creating minor floods. So I decided that I would continue to use it. But I wasn't about to let the other guys in on it, since I was afraid that too much traffic there might spoil it for us.

The new piss room was set up, and I democratically used it a couple of times and it worked pretty well—for about two days. Then we started to learn about the property of some two gallons of urine and how it affected and was affected by an unventilated room. Then, and only then, did we truly realize the fatal flaw in Hughes's plan: There was no provision for getting rid of the stuff. We decided, though, that we'd just have to solve this one without Hughes's help. (God only knows what he would have suggested we do with the stuff.)

Just outside the door that led to the parking lot was a storm drain that had been placed there to dispose of rainwater that fell on the entire lot. We decided that we would use the buckets during the day, and at the first sign of darkness (late, because it was summer) we'd empty those buckets into the drain. I shouldn't say "we" when

I talk about the emptying detail. I pulled rank: After all, wasn't *I* the only one to be there *all the time* with Hughes? And that should entitle me not to have to dump buckets of urine while worrying that the famous pop composer upstairs or one of his guests might notice what was happening under their (I can't resist it) very noses.

With this problem solved, life settled down to an extraordinarily boring routine. Perhaps this can best be described by going through a typical day:

8:00 A.M. Hughes kicked on the door. I opened it and he went into the john, leaving the door open. He sat on the toilet for a couple of hours. (His diet was causing incredible constipation, which should have come as no surprise to anyone: When you eat nothing but chocolate bars and nuts and wash it down with milk and some Poland Water, you'll be lucky to fart, much less find anything to crap out.) Afterwards he spent ten minutes throwing water over his head and upper body, and after that he took another ten minutes to comb his still-wet hair until it was plastered flat against his head. He combed it straight back, by the way. Then he went back into the theater. (During this period spent in the bathroom he had not spoken to either of the men sitting in that lobby, not an unusual occurrence. Often days would pass without his speaking to any one of us at Nosseck's.)

12:00 noon. Hughes walked to the back of the theater and made a phone call from the instrument there. From the projection booth I could hear him asking for messages, so it was safe to assume that he was calling Operations. Then he went back to his chair and stretched out as if trying to sleep.

3:00 P.M. Another kick on the door. He walked through the lobby and went into the bathroom. More time on the throne, more water splashed on himself, more hair combing, then back into the theater. Inside he played with his Kleenex boxes for the next two hours.

7:30 P.M. A short phone call, followed by a signal to Carl to come down into the theater. Carl went inside, listened to Hughes's instructions, and left the theater. As he went back to the projection booth, he said, "Showtime." At hearing this welcome news both Lloyd and I made a mad dash for the booth. As soon as Carl had the projectors fired up he'd start running the film that had been selected by Hughes. We were rapturously grateful for even the rottenest movie: It was the only time that time itself seemed to pass quickly. (While this left the lobby unguarded, no one had been trying to get in the doors except Johnnie and the drivers bringing food for us.) Whenever Hughes would wave his arms, the screening would end. This movie he watched from beginning to end, and it was a long one, thank heaven.

11:30 P.M. With the movie ended, it was back into the toilet for Hughes. A short session: just a splash bath and a quick comb-out. Then back into the theater.

12:20 A.M. A knock on the door. Johnnie Holmes arrived, evidently on orders placed in that evening call, with Hughes's food. He would always bring the old ice bucket out with him.

6:30 A.M. Hughes finally finished his banquet. The time spent eating was about four hours, for an amount of food that anyone else could put away in about 15 minutes.

7:00 A.M. A kick on the door. Hughes came out of the theater and went into the john, to sit on the crapper for two hours. After that it was water on himself, hair combing, and a silent retreat to the pleasures of the Kleenex boxes.

While Hughes was spending *his* time in such an interesting fashion, *my* days were even more dramatic. I sat a lot. I fought with Lloyd or Fred over who would get use of the couch. I called my wife on the pay phone. I went into the projection booth and ordered food. I walked out into the parking lot during the daytime and talked with Willie, the black dude who kept peace in the parking lot behind the building. I'd try and enjoy the outside world. Then I'd go back inside and sit some more. My time was occupied perhaps 30 minutes out of every 24 hours.

There was, obviously, a lot of time left for me to wonder why I was there. Lloyd, Fred, and I spent a lot of time sitting and talking. We covered almost every topic known to man. But the one thing that was almost conspicuous by its absence was the basic question: What are we doing here? I don't think any of us wanted to explore that. I know I didn't want to talk about it. The reason I was there could well have stood for the other guys. It was simple. First, I was in awe of Hughes. He was by far the most complicated personality I had ever met.

But there was a deeper, darker secret: I wanted his money. Not all of it, you understand, but only a few million to keep me cooking until I could figure out what it was I *really* wanted to do with my life.

Obviously, to get that money one had to be *with Hughes*. It seemed only possible. After all, he had a wife, but he had no children and no brothers or sisters. In fact, he had no other living relatives that I had heard of. But he did have hundreds and hundreds of millions of dollars. Since he couldn't take it with him and since it seemed vulgar to leave it *all*—every last dime—to his widow, it was not inconceivable, in the wide world of daydreams, that some small portion of that money could be left for his faithful Tonto, good old Ron Kistler. (This greed factor is something that could well be raised with any number of Hughes's employees.)

My fantasy of Hughes touching me with his golden wand was wearing a bit thin, though, as I sat it out at Nosseck's. I might have taken the hike I had been thinking about had not Hughes made me do one thing that so captured my interest that I had a folding bed sent in and placed in the second cutting room, so that I wouldn't have to sleep on the couch. Hughes got me when he called me into the theater and asked me to take some dictation.

Chapter 10

When Hughes asked me to take some dictation, I was mightily surprised. His Operations staff, after all, was made up of men who could take dictation at astounding rates of speed and type nearly as fast. Neither skill had been emphasized in the schools of Monte Vista, Colorado, but my boss had asked me to do something and so I prepared to do it. I went into the lobby and came back with a legal-sized, ruled notebook that was part of a stack of such notebooks I hadn't noticed before. Perhaps Holmes had brought them in on his last food run.

Hughes began dictating a letter that had to do with the affairs of TWA. It was to be sent to someone who seemed to want Hughes not to be involved in the running of the airline. The dictation was a three-page, single-spaced letter, and I was told to put a copy of it in a safe place so that *I* could refer to it later. Because the letter was a recitation of the performance of TWA, and Hughes's relation to it, I felt more a part of Hughes's important work than I ever had.

Later, of course, I was to wish that I had had access to a photocopying machine, because it turned out that I was sitting in the middle of one of the greatest dramas in

American corporate history. But at the time I was like an infantryman who can s? only what he can see and has no real grasp of the overall implications of what is going on.

All of us who worked for Hughes Productions knew that *something* big was happening. For one thing, our work at 7000 Romaine had been under the scrutiny of reporters and photographers from *Fortune* magazine who had been lurking around, watching what we did, preparing a story on Hughes and TWA. (The photographers had taken to parking on Romaine in the block west of the building. With long lenses they had a perfect view of the Operations window that was used for transmitting messages. This horrified the staff people, who would lean out of the window to see a 500-mm lens pointing their way.)

A quick look at the financial magazines would tell anyone that TWA and Howard Hughes were having big problems. Hughes owned over 78 percent of the airline, and he treated it as his own. We knew that the pilots and other personnel connected with the actual flying of the planes loved Hughes, with *his* encyclopedic knowledge of flying; but he must have been a nightmare for the marketing people. Every time we would go down to the airport and roll out a red carpet for someone that Operations had decreed was a VIP, we had to be angering the rest of the passengers in the plane—not because one of them was someone special, but because the pomp associated with getting this one person off the plane delayed the other passengers from disembarking.

But the question of the distribution of favors wasn't the issue causing all the flak at TWA and with Hughes. It was, of course, a matter of money.

The first all-jet aircraft were about to roll off the assembly lines at Boeing and Douglas and Convair. Everyone thought that they would revolutionize air travel, and every airline had committed itself to choosing one brand or another. The problem of financing fleets of new equipment and the ground support systems that were needed to handle the planes and their passengers had been an item of importance equal to the question of which planes to buy.

TWA's crisis was that it had not lined up financing. Or rather Hughes hadn't. Although Hughes held no position in the TWA corporate hierarchy (for that matter, he didn't even sit on the board of directors), he had committed the airline to the purchase of 63 jet airplanes (Boeing 707s and Convair 880s). The price tag for the airplanes and spare engines was around $415 million.

It was money Hughes didn't have. And Hughes was not of a disposition often seen, or liked, by bankers or other large lenders. He didn't like having partners. He liked working out of his own head, free from all the support systems (he would call them restraints, and on that he and the lenders would agree) common to business.

Hughes called me into the theater and asked me to record some notes for him. He gave me the name of the head of the First of Boston (I was later to learn that this man, George Woods, was head of the First Boston Corporation) and a long list of requests to be made to this man.

Essentially, I wrote the following notes: "Hughes would like to talk to your firm about the borrowing of a large sum of money. But before he can do that, certain precautions have to be taken at your end. After you hang up from this call we ask that you have your telephone line checked to make certain that there are no listening devices attached to the line. Secrete yourself in a private office that has been electronically swept for listening devices. Make sure that all doors and windows are securely closed. Make no mention of this call to anyone unless it is entirely necessary, and then only after swearing them to utter secrecy. Keep the number of such participants to a bare minimum. You will be given the names of parties who will represent Howard Hughes. You may discuss this matter with them, but with no one else, no matter what his position, in the Hughes organization."

There were a number of other stipulations, but they all came to the same thing: Woods and the First Boston Corporation were going to work in an atmosphere that would have done the CIA proud. It took hours to get the dictation exactly right, as I had to keep revising sections and then rereading the document to the Old Man.

Then it was time to implement this piece of paper. I was instructed to take the notes into the projection booth and to sit where I could see into the studio. There was a telephone in the booth, an extension of the one Hughes used. I was to pick up my phone on a signal from Hughes. I was then to read the message I had into the phone. I was to read slowly, distinctly, and to be certain that the party on the other end understood completely.

Hughes picked up his phone, dialed a number, and waited for an answer. I could see him talking to someone, and then he pointed a finger at me. I picked up my phone and started giving instructions to the party at the other end. I was nervous, but not worried, because Hughes stayed on the line. (I knew that he'd bail me out in *this* situation if I needed it.) The voice at the other end of the line indicated that he understood the requests and that they could all be met.

After enough time had passed that all the security

procedures could be implemented in Boston, Hughes called back and took over. The amount of money in question, I found, was $268 million. When I heard that I was glad that Hughes had decided to carry the ball himself. It was not a sum that I would have been comfortable talking about, not after just barely qualifying for a Sears's charge account.

As I said, being a spear carrier in the Hughes scheme of things, it was difficult for me to understand the full implications of what Hughes was doing. (It was getting difficult for the supposed honchos in Operations, too. As our time wore on at Nosseck's, Hughes began to call in less and less. In fact, I started to receive calls on the Nosseck wire from staff, asking me what the Old Man was up to: Who had he called? What had he said? I couldn't fill them in on the details. Through the thin walls of the studio I could hear Hughes's side of telephone conversations, but not the other—even allowing for the fact that Hughes was holding the earpiece of the phone not tight against his ear but close to the mike of his hearing aid.)

Whatever he was doing regarding TWA, it was at the cost of any semblance of personal order. He had achieved a degree of body odor not acceptable in modern American society. Worse, the residue from his "showers" had built up on his shirt until it looked like a modern painting, done in grime. His trousers, too, had been hit with some of the spray and were stained with several water marks. The result was that one of America's richest men looked absolutely down and out: He could have blended in on any skid row in the nation.

Apparently the situation finally got to him. He called me into the theater, gave me one of his imploring looks, and said, "Ron, my shirt and trousers are in dire need of cleaning. Do you think you could clean them up for me?"

I gave them a long, careful look and gave him my emphatic answer: "No!"

Hughes is not a man who gives up easily when he wants something. "Don't you think," he asked, "that you could get a can of cleaning fluid and take the biggest stains off? You should be able to clean them up real well with cleaning fluid."

I wanted no part of this. "There is," I said, "no way in this world that those clothes could be cleaned. They are so old and dirty that they would fall apart when exposed to a cleaning solvent."

Hughes's face twisted in pain. He sat for several minutes in silence. Then he tried again.

"Ron, this is my favorite outfit." No shit. I had never seen him wear anything else. "Won't you at least give it a try?"

Perhaps I had won a victory. He was *asking*, not *telling*, me to do that disgusting job. But I was not going to give ground.

"There is no way to clean those clothes. You are just going to have to throw them away and get some clean ones."

At that he sent me out of the theater. Two hours later he summoned me back inside.

"Ron, are you *sure*—" I met this with a vigorous shake of my head. "Very well, then," said Hughes, "if we can't clean them, we'll just have to throw them away."

He stood up and began to unbutton his shirt. When he had finished he shrugged his shoulders and the shirt fell to the floor. Then he unbuckled his belt, unzipped his fly, and let his tan gabardine slacks slide to his ankles. There he stood in all his glory—his white-on-white frail body was unencumbered by any underwear. It was truly a sight to behold.

Howard Hughes, whose Tool Company and Aircraft Company were worth around $580 million (according to *Fortune*, and it is important to remember that Hughes had *given* the Aircraft Company, which was involved in scientific R&D, to the Howard Hughes Medical Institute, of which he was sole trustee; while this meant he still had strong ties to that corporate enterprise, he couldn't use it for his own purposes the way he used the Tool Company), stood in front of me, stark naked. The man who owned 78 percent of Trans World Airlines, the man who was in dire need of $250 million or so in cash to pay for jet planes, hadn't had a shave or haircut in God knows how many months. His gray-white beard fell six inches down on his chest and the hair on the back of his head was almost to his shoulders. There was only one thing that could be called impressive about Hughes at that moment: sexually, he was very well endowed.

He stepped out of his trousers, leaned over, and picked them and his shirt off the floor. But before I could take those grubby garments away from him, he pulled them back as if he'd had a change of heart. Then he began a frantic search of the rear pockets of the trousers. The left one was empty. He put his hand in the right one and immediately began to smile. He withdrew his hand and I could see a small piece of crumpled paper in his fingers.

Hughes shoved his clothes under his arm and began to work over that small piece of paper with both hands. He unfolded and smoothed out the paper until it was finally possible to identify the thing: It was a five-dollar bill, one that was so damned old, worn, and mildewed that it had lost about 90 percent of its original green color. But it *was* legal tender.

"See, Ron," Hughes fairly cackled, "I'm not broke yet.

I still have five dollars to my name. Don't you worry about the Old Man; he's still got money." At that he dissolved in laughter, and so did I. The world might think that Howard Hughes was in a bad way (especially if they could *see* him just then), his financial men might think he was up against it, but Howard Hughes and Ron Kistler knew that at least he wasn't tapped out. Hell, he had five bucks.

When we stopped laughing I held out my hand for the clothes, and he slowly handed them to me. I took them, walked out to the lobby, and deposited the garments into a large waste container. I swear that as he handed those clothes to me there were tears in his eyes, but maybe they came from laughing.

The next day Johnnie Holmes arrived at Nosseck's with a package that looked like a shirt box from a laundry. He went into the theater, stayed only a few moments, and then came out without the box. I hurried into the projection booth to see what had been delivered. Hughes was standing in the theater, a vision in a clean white shirt. Granted, the shirt looked to be a size that would have accommodated someone 100 pounds heavier than Hughes, and there were still no trousers, but it was a definite improvement. For walking around, his outfit was completed by his brown wing-tips, still with no laces. Howard Hughes was ready for the Easter Parade.

Just about the only continuing amusement Hughes provided came during his increasingly infrequent phone calls to the Major or the Party. Sitting in the theater, he would bounce around on the couch next to the phone and do one thing I found wonderous to behold: Hughes was able to cross all his toes, one over the other, starting at the outside and working his way in to the big toe. What made it special was that he did it without using his hands.

(One day Dick Homer came by to deliver some food to me. I shushed Dick, took him into the projection booth, and pointed towards Hughes's seated ballet. Homer got so hysterical and laughed so loud that Hughes, as hard of hearing as he was, started twisting around to see what was making that terrible noise.)

We had to create our own amusement out in the lobby, so we assembled a healthy hobby and crafts department. We brought in cards, jigsaw puzzles, crossword puzzles, paint-by-numbers sets, and anything else the hobby shops offered by way of time-and-brain consumers. Our paperback library was extensive, we brought in a small portable radio, and we were trying to figure out where to put a TV set.

All this stuff was necessary not only because it was downright boring being there (most of the time), but Hughes himself was getting testier and testier. One day he issued the edict that he simply didn't want any of us to talk to him. Well, we weren't exactly beating our gums whenever he was around. What he wanted now, though, was absolute silence. Perhaps he was punishing us for the faint noise of the radio that might trickle in through the wall and his impaired hearing. Perhaps he was pissed because although we were polite enough to cover our steaming meals whenever he walked through as we were eating, we could cover the food but not the smell of it.

Hughes might have been carrying around the awful memory of a smell that he felt he had no right to smell. During the great toilet dilemma, I had in disgust one day decided to urinate without turning to the overflowing buckets and without racing upstairs. I decided that what was good enough for Howard Hughes was good enough for Ron Kistler. But I had reckoned without the casual habits of Hughes when in a toilet. He had let fly in so many directions and had put down so much paper to cover his bad aim that the few steps to the can would have been on ten layers of soggy paper. But I was not to be denied, so I unzipped and let go in the sink.

Sure enough, within half an hour Hughes bounded out of the theater and headed for the bathroom. There was an awful howl. He came out to confront three men—we all happened to be there—who were all trying to keep a very stiff upper lip.

"Someone has pissed in my sink!" he raged.

Dead silence. He growled and raged, and I must say that those other guys were terrific in taking a berating that was rightfully only mine. After a while, Hughes ran out of steam and stalked off to do his business in the toilet. It was one of the rare occasions when he was mean —and justified, although I *would* argue that any normal plan for our toilet habits would have prevented my awful lapse from ever occurring.

But Hughes always found a way to attempt to make up for being impossible to get along with. For example, one day he asked Fred to stay when Lloyd came on duty and for the three of us to come into the theater. When we got there we were directed to stand, side by side, about five feet from the ottoman. We knew it was going to be a hearts-and-flowers speech. He had delivered them before, and this one was long overdue: Hughes had been acting like an utter asshole for the past couple of days— snapping at us as he passed—and he knew it as well as we did.

"Just stand where you are, fellows," he said. "And remember not to talk. Please don't move about as I'm speaking. Just relax and stay put." Damn! He couldn't even let us act like human beings when he was going to give us a line of bullshit.

"I want to tell you fellows how much I appreciate having you here with me. It means so much to me to have you here and see how well you do your jobs. I'll make all of this up to you someday.

"You'll see that I haven't forgotten all the things you've done to make it easier for me. I know that you're all working longer hours than you'd like to, but I just can't let any of you go or take my chances with a new man. We won't be here—"

Just then I made a sudden move that carried me past his chair, to a point about ten feet behind him. It violated his regulations, but I thought what I was about to do would be more important. I stomped my foot up and down and then slowly returned to my place with Fred and Lloyd. Hughes hadn't been able to see what I was doing because the back of his chair had blocked his view. I stood there, grinning. Hughes was not smiling at all.

"Ron, I asked you not to move. You know better than to move that quickly when you are in my room." I kept on grinning.

"What caused you to go back there so quickly? Did you *see* something?" I made an elaborate yes nod with my head.

"What did you see? A fly?"

I shook my head no.

"A moth?"

No.

"A cockroach?"

No.

"A spider?"

No.

"Well, if you didn't see any of those insects, what *did* you see?"

I wished that I had spent more of my party time learning the nuances of charades. The Old Man had asked a question and wanted an answer, but he didn't want me to speak. I started wiggling my thumbs and fingers after arranging them to indicate that they were supposed to represent a body.

"Ron, did you see a *frog?*"

I went back into the act and tried to indicate that Hughes was getting warm.

"Ron, did you see a *lizard?*"

I damned near jumped up and down in joy. "Yes," I nodded vigorously. I had indeed seen a six-inch lizard, which had had the unmitigated gall to walk across the floor not ten feet from the world's foremost hater of subhuman species. Not only had I seen the lizard—I'd killed the brazen sonofabitch. I was grinning so broadly I thought I'd split a lip. Hughes couldn't get over it.

"Ron, you mean you saw a lizard, and that you *killed* it?" Yeah! I just kept nodding. I fear that anyone looking in from the projection booth would have thought I was auditioning for the part Dwight Frye played in *Dracula*— the real-estate agent who went nuts after a little necking with Bela Lugosi and then began begging for flies.

Hughes began to smile. "You know," he said, *"I've* seen that lizard in here. More than once, in fact. But I didn't dare tell you fellows, 'cause I knew what you'd have thought."

He was so right. If he'd told any of us that he'd started seeing a lizard prancing around we'd have called for the psychiatric pick-up truck. This distraction, though, was enough to call a halt to the rest of his speech, which was just as well. We'd heard it before.

Chapter 11

As the summer wore on, I managed one great feat of protection for Howard Hughes. It came about because of the matter of Eddie Fisher's air conditioner.

Fisher had taken a lease on the penthouse of Nosseck's building and was about to have the offices redone. It had gotten warm, and Fisher and his people wanted to have air conditioners put into his suite. Unfortunately for them, those window-type air conditioners pulled so much power that some adjustments had to be made in the building's master box.

That box was located in the first cutting room in Nosseck's (a/k/a the piss room). The first I knew of their problem was when a couple of electricians came down and knocked on the door that led to the parking lot. I went out and they asked if they could come in and hook up a couple of wires that would equalize the load running through the box. Naturally, I couldn't let them in.

It didn't take much thinking to know that this could easily become a very ugly situation, and one in which we had a very shaky piece of ground to stand on. Because I wasn't permitted to speak to Hughes, I called Operations and outlined the problem. Operations called

Hughes. Hughes said, no entrance. Operations called me, and said don't let them pass.

So I looked out our little window and there would be the building owner, Fisher's agent, and Fisher's attorney; they'd be standing out there in the heat, and all they wanted to do was hook up two wires. I volunteered to do it for them, but that wouldn't make it.

The climax came when I heard some terrible beating on the door. It was in the afternoon, and Hughes just happened to be sitting on the toilet, about three feet from that door. I looked out and the usual cast of would-be enterers—the owner, Fisher's agent, Fisher's attorney, a couple of electricians—had been joined by a guy in a uniform. The uniformed guy was a county sheriff (the Sunset Strip is unincorporated county land, not part of the City of Los Angeles), and he was waving a piece of paper that looked suspiciously legal.

Hughes started hollering at me from the toilet. "What do they want?" Naturally I had to break the silence he had imposed on us to tell him that they wanted in, and not only that, they had the legal *right* to get in. Hughes had an answer for that: "Keep 'em out!"

So I went outside and faced the assembled group. I figured that none of them knew who was inside or what was going on (a long time later I heard that Martin Nosseck's cover story as to who was using his studio to the exclusion of his show-biz customers was that the Atomic Energy Commission had taken the place over to work on a secret government film about the atomic bomb). So, mostly in desperation, I told them that they didn't have any idea of what they were up against or what was going on inside. There was something in there, I said, that was bigger than they were, and bigger than their court order. And if they doubted that, I suggested that they check with the local office of the FBI. And with that I walked back inside.

The damnedest thing was that they bought it. They all left. But I knew that they'd be back, and soon, and when they came there'd be no bullshit story that would keep them out.

My inventiveness dearly pleased Hughes, sitting there on the throne. He wanted to know what I'd said, and when I told him he broke out in laughter. It was one of the few good laughs he had while trying to move his bowels. He had already taken over Nosseck's private office as the Howard Hughes enema center. But on his diet, nothing was going to help. On one occasion he sat on the toilet, in that tiny area that gave him about as much legroom as you get in the back seat of a sports car, for *26 consecutive hours,* groaning and rocking back and forth. While he was in there, *I* was right outside the open door, sitting on a film can, taking dictation about TWA in between his futile attempts to accomplish his mission.

Hughes's inability to take a decent dump was only the most dramatic manifestation of the deterioration of his physical condition. His diet had taken its toll. When he walked into Nosseck's he had been 6'3" and perhaps 155 pounds. After a couple of months of his Hershey bar-pecan-milk-Poland Water diet, he was down to around 100 pounds.

His bones seemed to be trying to cut through his flesh: there was no cushion of fat to impede them. His cheekbones were grotesquely out of proportion to the rest of his sunken face. The black circles under his eyes appeared to be the work of a makeup artist trying to recapture the look of Lon Chaney in *The Phantom of the Opera.* His calves looked like wrists, and his thighs were the size of healthy forearms. His buttocks had lost so much flesh that there were several rolls of loose skin piled one on top of the other. (This resulted in Lloyd, Fred, and I calling him "Saddlebags.") His color was bad and his temperament was worse.

I had become truly concerned about his health—mental as well as physical. He seemed to be lapsing into extended periods of irrationality. (Since then I've done some reading and can't help guessing that his diet was the primary cause of this.) I decided that Operations had to be told what was going on. I called Kay Glenn.

"Kay," I said, "I'm afraid the Old Man is going to die." There was a long, long silence.

Finally Glenn was able to rasp, "Ron, what makes you think that?"

I told him about Hughes's diet, his toilet habits, his sleeping conditions, his loss of weight, and his lack of adequate bathing facilities. Kay was upset, and upset with me for not telling him about any of this earlier. He instructed me to call Bill Gay and repeat my story.

When I called Gay I repeated the details and was instructed to wait by the phone for an important call. A short time later the phone rang. It was a man who identified himself as a doctor. I had to repeat the whole story to him and was asked a series of questions having to do with skin color, respiration, speech coherence, firmness of step, mental alertness, and so on. Well, if the doctor had a line on what the problem was, the real question was what was he going to do about it. He couldn't very well call Hughes to the phone and tell him that he was sick. That decision would be made by Hughes and no one else. We did decide that I would call Operations every day with a report on Hughes's well-being. I suggested that a standby team of doctors, nurses, and an ambulance be held at the ready, but I don't know whether it was done.

I was not the only one who thought Hughes might be very ill. He was calling the Major and the Party less and less often, but when he did he went into a routine that was astonishing, so much so that Fred, Lloyd, and I spent hours piecing the thing together and making sure that we had heard what we thought we had heard. What Hughes was doing when he talked to those two women was to convince them that he was seriously ill and *was in a hospital.*

My first tip-off to this came one night when I was sitting in the theater, waiting to take dictation. Hughes got on the phone and called his wife. I paid little attention to what he was saying until I heard him say, "Nurse Hannah is with me now and is preparing to give me a bath."

As he said that he looked straight at me. Now, I'm a lot of things, but my name isn't Hannah and I'm not a nurse. The whole episode was so damned odd that I didn't mention it to Fred or Lloyd. A couple of days later, though, I was in the room and he was on the phone.

"Nurse Hannah just came in the room," Hughes said, and as I stared at him he gave me that same look he had given me a couple of days earlier when he had identified me as the mystery nurse. "She's about to give me an enema." I looked around for the nurse or at least for the enema bag. But it was just Hughes and Kistler. When I left the room I felt compelled to ask Lloyd and Fred about this: Was *I* going *nuts* or was it Saddlebags? Both of them were relieved to hear my questions and account of what had happened.

They were quick to volunteer that they were apparently Nurse Grace and Nurse Sarah. Nurse Grace seemed to specialize in intravenous feedings while Nurse Sarah was the expert in taking readings of blood pressure. Grace, Sarah, and Hannah were all quite competent, and Hughes had been heard telling the Major *and* the Party that he was going to do something nice for the nurses when he left the hospital.

Not only did he *tell* the two women that he wasn't well, he *sounded* it. He got weaker and weaker with every passing day—or at least his voice did. He explained to the Major and the Party that he was losing strength and that a vast army of doctors was unable to pinpoint the problem. (Since Hughes loathed the medical profession, this particular lie must have come readily to his lips.) As the summer wore on he became so feeble when talking to the ladies that it must have been obvious to them that he was at death's door. Often, though, he'd forget that he had hung up the phone, that the act was over, and he'd continue it while talking to me. As he whispered at me I'd just put my hand up to my ear to indicate that his Camille routine was working—I couldn't hear him. His recovery would be immediate and total: he'd continue speaking, but in a normal tone of voice.

One thing that he was able to accomplish by all this was to confine all his calls to *his* schedule. The women understood that because he was so terribly ill, there could be no incoming calls. Whenever Hughes felt like it, *he* called *them*. However sick Hughes *actually* was, he *was* in control.

Another thing he always seemed in control of was our relationship. Whenever I was particularly angry at him, he'd always sense it and choose that time to apologize to me for the strain he was putting me under. The most extraordinary example of this sensitivity on his part came approximately two hours after I had called Operations to tell them that I thought the Old Man was dying.

Hughes called me into the theater and asked me to get the legal tablet that contained some of his previous dictation. Specifically, he wanted me to find that first dictation about TWA, that complex three-plus pages he had dictated almost two months earlier.

"Follow along on your notes," Hughes said, once I had located the notebook and returned to the theater, "and see if I remember this thing correctly." With that he began, from memory, to repeat each and every word that I had written down. I sat in awe, reading along, as he redictated the document, word for word, paragraph for paragraph, as he had before. (If our current memory expert, ex-basketball player Jerry Lucas, could have been there he would have given Hughes a medal.)

At the conclusion of the document, Hughes said, "Well, Ron, did I get it right?" I was much too dumbfounded to say anything. All I could do was shake my head in the affirmative. Looking at him, I got his message: Mind your own damned business and don't ever think for an instant that Howard Hughes isn't in control of the situation. If he seems to be doing things *you* don't understand, rest assured that *he* understands them.

The next time I spoke to Operations, to give them my Hughes health report, I found that I just couldn't be as emphatic about his condition as I had the day before.

If they had bothered to ask about *my* health, though, I would have given them an earful. Notwithstanding my quick trips home, I was feeling the difficulty of the duty at Nosseck's. After all, my marriage was being severely tested by my absence. I called Virgie whenever I could, but she wasn't too interested in my calls. Nor was she enthusiastic when I arrived home in a cloud of dust, jumped into the bath, cleaned myself up, and raced back to Nosseck's. (Even the dalliances weren't as joyous as they might have been).

I needed to be able to spend some time at home. That required a plan. The plan wasn't brilliant—it just needed some good acting on my part. I knew very well that the Old Man was deathly afraid of colds, pneumonia, any disease that had to do with the respiratory system. Anyone who sneezed or coughed in his presence would be sent from the room immediately until it could be determined that he was not ill. So I made a date with my wife and started my act.

The next time I was summoned into the theater by Hughes I stood in front of his chair, as always, waiting for him to acknowledge my presence. When he looked at me I allowed my knees to sag ever so slightly, brushed my forehead with my hand, and in general tried to look like someone who had narrowly avoided keeling over.

"Ron, are you feeling well? Tell me."

"No," I replied. "I don't feel well at all." He seemed to shrink back into his chair.

"Are you coming down with a cold?"

"No," I said. "But I seem to have picked up a headache I can't shake." That was all it took.

"You've had a long spell here, Ron," Hughes said. "I think that you had better go on home, have a good rest, and take care of yourself. Stay there until you hear from me."

I got my stuff together and got out. It was just short of three months that I spent with Hughes at Nosseck's. I spent a couple of weeks getting reacquainted with my wife and kids, all at full salary, except that full salary meant $80 a week.

A few days after I left Nosseck's, Hughes left, too,

returning to his bungalow at the Beverly Hills Hotel. I went back to the drivers' room after two weeks and resumed my duties as head of the drivers. Then I got another call from Kay Glenn. I was to report to the Beverly Hills Hotel. The Old Man wanted me.

Chapter 12

Virgie wasn't overjoyed at the thought of my leaving for another tour of duty with a man who had demonstrated his indifference to my home life. But Kay had said nothing that would indicate I'd be staying at the hotel; of course he wouldn't. Even assuming that I was to stay around the hotel, it was a shorter drive from our house in the San Fernando Valley, over Coldwater Canyon, than it was into Hollywood.

I had learned a lesson from the Nosseck's tour. When I left my house I had with me a two-suiter crammed full of clothes as well as a toilet kit. Oh, yes—I also took along two fifths of Jim Beam. I didn't know if Carl would be at the hotel and I therefore couldn't count on his supply of Early Times.

The drive to the hotel was a transition from middle-class America to the world of the newly made rich. That section of the Los Angeles hills is filled with houses built by movie money. It's an area where you *pray* you'll be rear-ended in your car: Whatever hits you will be rich and *very* insured. The Beverly Hills Hotel was and is one of the symbols of that kind of wealth. The hotel was built around 1912 as a splendid resort, midway between Los

Angeles and the ocean. The city, of course, grew towards the west, and the independent community of Beverly Hills was founded, primarily to provide an exclusive area for movie people to live in. The owners of the hotel have modernized it over the years, but it still carries about it vestiges of the *kind* of elegance that is most often associated with the forties.

Kay had told me to check with the assistant manager of the hotel, and when I did, the man seemed to be expecting me. He immediately took me to the second floor and showed me a room. It was smaller than I expected at such a posh hotel, but it was nicely furnished. What really turned my head, though, was the huge basket of fresh fruit that had been put on a coffee table. As I was strictly a cheap-motel guy, this welcoming touch knocked me out. So, for that matter, did the rate card on the door. It said that that little room was going for $36 a day. It made me thankful that I hadn't signed a registration card: At least I couldn't be named as an accessory to charges like those. I unpacked and put my Sears shorts and Fruit of the Loom tee shirts into drawers.

Being cautious, I walked the corridors to fix the locations of fire escapes, stairs, and other exits, although with the elevator right next to my room, I probably wouldn't have use for any other mode of transportation. Then I went back to my room and started reading the room-service menu. The phone rang. It was Jack Eggers, a Hughes employee who was staying at the hotel. He told me that Hughes wanted me to report to Bungalow Four at once. Jack said that he would meet me there.

Of course, I had no idea where Bungalow Four was. I went downstairs and began wandering the grounds. The Beverly Hills Hotel, like the Ambassador and the Chateau Marmont in L.A., has used its grounds not only for the obvious swimming pool and gardens, but also to provide cottages for guests who don't want to have to worry about hearing some drunk standing in the hall at 3:00 A.M., looking for his keys. Theoretically, the only wrinkle a bungalow will ever put into a guest's nose occurs when an errant, if expensive, leaf falls onto the room-service cart as it's being wheeled from the kitchen.

The bungalows at the Beverly Hills Hotel were on the northern part of the grounds (the hotel's main building faced Sunset Boulevard from behind a moat of greenery, a driveway, and parking areas). I wandered around for a while, looking for the elusive number Four, which turned out to be nearest the hotel. (It was also near a walkway that led east to the public sidewalks on Crescent Drive. It was, therefore, possible to exit without going through the hotel lobby.)

Eggers seemed a little out of sorts when I finally found him. He gave me a hurried version of the laws concerning my entrance to, and exits from, the bungalow. We were standing in a low-walled patio. The architecture of the building was a vaguely Spanish style that is well-known in L.A. The roof was covered with red tile. Get in and out *fast,* Eggers was saying. Then he grabbed a fold-ed-up newspaper and started fanning vigorously at the door. I was to see this repeated hundreds of times, but that first glimpse caused me to think that Eggers was auditioning for the funny farm.

"Get ready," he said.

I moved as close as I could to the door without putting myself in range to be swatted by his newspaper. Eggers had the newspaper in one hand and a Kleenex covering the other. Using that Kleenex-covered hand, he grabbed the doorknob, twisted it open, and created about a 12-inch space for me to squeeze through. I jumped into the gloom, and Eggers shut the door behind me.

"Just stand right there and don't move, Ron. And remember not to talk." I recognized the voice of Howard Hughes. I stood, waiting for my eyes to adjust to the darkness of the room. When they did, I was glad that Hughes had had me stop in my tracks. One step in any direction and I would have tripped over something. Hughes had transformed the living room of an expensive suite in an expensive hotel into something that looked like a movie set meant to represent an artist's garret.

The room was about 15 by 24 feet. Against one wall was a fireplace, framed by smoky, gold-veined mirrored squares. The hotel furniture, elegant yet comfortable, consisted of a large, overstuffed couch, two small matching chairs, an overstuffed love seat, several end tables, and a couple of coffee tables.

Whoever had furnished that room hadn't known that Howard Hughes was going to stay there. Edgar Albert Guest once said that "It takes a heap of living to make a house a home." Hughes had done his best for the "heap" part of that thought. He had added his big leather chair and ottoman to the room, putting them in the center. To make space, the hotel's furniture had been pushed to the sides of the room.

It wasn't only a matter of making a place for two pieces of Hughes furnishings. On coffee tables two 35-mm movie projectors had been set up. Behind them was a wrought-iron patio chair, armless, with a small cushion on the seat and another cushion on the back. Both of those cushions were themselves cushioned by an accumulation of birdshit. There was a large movie screen in front of Hughes's chair, and near it a large speaker box. Approximately 20 full-size film cans (holding standard movie reels) were spread out in rows on the floor, laid out so as to make narrow paths to various sections of the room. Stacks of newspapers and magazines were piled all around.

In the small open spaces between the furniture, film cans, and piles of reading materials, there were mounds of wadded-up tissues, mute testimony to Hughes's unceasing use of the Kleenex to ward off evil (a/k/a germs), as well as to provide an outlet for his nervous energy.

Having looked the room over, I searched out Hughes. He had given up on the costume I had left him in at Nosseck's—the shirt flapping around his buttocks and the shoes. Rather, he had half-given it up. The shoes remained, but he had dispensed with the shirt. For the sake of modesty, he had covering his groin a large pink napkin of the sort furnished by the Beverly Hills Hotel to people eating in its restaurants. His hair and beard hadn't been trimmed since I had last seen him.

But he had obviously eaten. He didn't appear nearly as gaunt as I remembered him. I was also pleased to note that his exposed skin had a healthy pinkish tinge that gave evidence of being recently bathed and rubbed down with a towel. I thought that Hughes might try some small talk, but that wasn't his way.

"Ron, that is your chair over there," he said, and with a sinking heart I glanced over to see that he *did* mean the birdshit-covered number. "Go sit in it and don't move around. You will find a book of instructions on how to run those projectors. Read it and make damned sure that you know how to operate them. It shouldn't take you that long considering the amount of time you've spent in the projection booth with Carl."

And I had thought that I was being circumspect in that projection booth! As I walked to my chair he had one more instruction for me.

"Remember! You are not to talk in this room. If you want to communicate with me you can write a note on one of the pads you'll find on the table. But I cannot imagine anything that would be important enough to require you to write me a note." It seemed to me that he was telling me that he didn't much care to hear from me.

I sat in the chair, found the instruction manual, and then did what I thought was a normal thing: I turned on a lamp so that I could better see the words I was supposed to be reading. You would have thought I had gotten up, run over to Hughes's chair, and sneezed directly in his face.

Hughes whipped around and positively growled at me. "Turn that damned light off. If I want you to turn the damned light on, I'll damned well tell you to turn the damned light on. Now turn the damned light *off*." So I squinted at the manual in light that would have given an owl a headache.

After *hours,* Hughes dismissed me from the bungalow and I went back to my room. I was dead tired and looking forward to a good sleep. After a quick shower I crawled into bed.

Buzz—whirr—clank! It sounded as if the hotel had rented out space to a boiler factory. I got out of bed, put on my pants, and went into the hall to find out what was making that noise. I didn't have to go far. One of my walls was the wall to the elevator shaft. I went back to my room, wrapped a pillow around my head, and finally fell asleep. I decided as I drifted off that my first task on awakening would be to find the manager and get my room changed.

The manager, however, chose that day to take off for parts unknown, or at least to make himself unavailable to me. But that wasn't the worst of it. After striking out on my would-be complaint, I dialed room service. When the ring was answered, I told the voice who I was, my room number, and without a pause launched into the breakfast that I wanted: a big glass of fresh orange juice, ham steak and four eggs, scrambled well, a double order of white toast, buttered well, cottage fried potatoes, a glass of milk, and coffee. After all, I hadn't had dinner the night before.

"I cannot take food orders from you, Mr. Kistler," the voice said. "You will have to order through Operations." Then there was a click on the line.

What? Instead of calling a kitchen perhaps a hundred yards from me to order food, I was supposed to call the Hughes number in *Hollywood?* More than a little pissed off, I was ready to do combat with Operations regarding my eating. As luck would have it, my call was taken by a man named Paul Wynn, to whom I had never cottoned.

"Paul," I said, gritting my teeth, "I've just tried to place a food order at the hotel and they wouldn't take it. They said I'd have to call Operations. What kind of shit is *that?*"

He was apparently ready for my call. "Ron," he said in that Utah twang that I had grown to hate, "Mr. Hughes has asked that you be placed on a restricted diet. You will have to place your food orders through this office so that we can make sure that you don't order anything that is prohibited."

"Bullshit!" I shouted. "I'm a free man, and I'm over twenty-one, and I'm fully capable of ordering my own meals!"

Wynn was obviously enjoying the conversation. "You will either have to order your food through this office," he said, "or go without eating." Well, it was difficult to serve two masters—Hughes and Operations—because you never *knew* whether rules had come from Hughes or from the clucks in Operations. Whenever I found that a law had been created by the toadies in Operations, I relished the opportunity to break it. But when something had been handed down by the Old Man, I intended to follow the rule—or at least be discreet in breaking it. I wasn't sure where this food rule came from.

The hunger pangs were raising hell with my stomach, so I played the game with Wynn. I settled for juice, oatmeal, toast, milk, and after a heated argument, coffee. (That argument convinced me that some of the food rules were not of Hughes's doing. The Mormon belief that its members shouldn't drink coffee was *their* belief, but I would be challenged on every occasion I ordered it at the hotel.)

After breakfast I went off to the bungalow after being called. When I got back to my room, the noise level from the elevator was intolerable. I stormed down to the desk and demanded someone in authority. I got the manager, and I told him that I wanted a new room—bigger *and* quieter. I figured that by then he would know that I was spending a lot of time in Bungalow Four. He dispatched a bellman to my room and told him to take my stuff to room 197. When I got to that room I found another bellman packing the belongings of another guest. He was out, I was in, and I could enjoy my own patio. I was especially proud that I had managed this switch in rooms without the assistance of Operations.

* * *

The people who were really helpful to me were Jack Eggers and his crew. They were known, collectively, as the "Third Man." They stayed in one of the smaller bungalows at the hotel. One of them was on duty at all times (occasionally all three would be called out for a job). Their first obligation was to the telephone in their bungalow; it was for the exclusive use of Howard Hughes. When he called them, he didn't want a busy signal.

Hughes used that phone as his version of room service. He would call for Poland Water, or food, or tell them to call me and have me come to his bungalow, or ask what time it was (and whether it was A.M. or P.M.) or if they had heard from the Major (Mrs. Hughes stayed in yet another bungalow at the hotel), or for any other assignment that he could dream up.

The best thing about these guys was that they, and I, were together in an undertaking that isolated us from most other people. We did loony things, at ridiculous hours, in all types of weather, often under the puzzled scrutiny of hotel employees and guests. We were often suffering great personal discomfort, all for the happiness of Howard Hughes. It was the kind of situation where men will band together, and we did just that. You really know who your friends are when you're standing together on the porch steps of Howard Hughes's bungalow from 1:00 A.M. till 5:30 A.M. in a driving California rainstorm.

One of the on-going jobs of Jack's crew was to deliver every edition of every local daily paper to Hughes as soon as it was delivered to the hotel. That was a fair amount of newsprint—three different papers with as many as five editions per day. Furthermore, it wasn't just a matter of buying a paper and carrying it over to Hughes's bungalow. In order to deliver *one* newspaper it was necessary to use *three* newspapers.

The Third Man would go and purchase, for example,

three copies of the *Times*'s street final. He would make certain that the folded edges of the three papers were exactly aligned and that the front pages were all facing up. Then he would go to the bungalow, brush away the flies, let himself in, and stand to one side of Hughes's chair.

Hughes would take a piece of Kleenex and use it to protect his hand. He'd take his covered hand, grasp the center paper of the three, and pull it out. The Third Man would take the other two papers and go back to his bungalow to wait for the next phone call from Hughes or the next new edition of a paper.

By following this procedure, the Third Man had a paper for the use of *his* bungalow for reading, a paper for use in shooing away flies from Hughes's front door, and —most important—Howard Hughes had avoided the germs that he knew lurked on the top and bottom paper.

It was Hughes's terror of germs that caused the Third Man to have to brush away the flies at the door to Hughes's bungalow before that door could be opened. (Whenever I was going to *leave* Hughes, a call would have to be made to the Third Man to get him in position for my exit.) Sometimes, though, the brushing at the flies wasn't as vigorous as it might have been. During the daytime, with hotel guests and others wandering the grounds, the fanning was done so quickly that I often failed to see it at all. You can imagine what a grown man felt like waving at real or imagined bugs. The guys would feel embarrassed if we had been involved in some grab-ass, and I cheered on their fanning with a loud, "Get him, Jack! Don't let him get *away!* Kill the sonofabitch!"

The Third Man crew was backstopped by Johnnie Holmes. With Hughes at Nosseck's and then at the hotel, there wasn't all that much driving for Holmes to do, but he continued to serve the Old Man in a number of ways. He was an integral part of Hughes's food-serving crew, coordinating the efforts of the waiters (both Hughes employees, not hotel; one of these men also served as cook) and the Third Man. Holmes was also a brilliant flycatcher, and would sometimes be called in when I wasn't in the bungalow (or was occupied with the projection machines) to rid the room of an insect that had evaded the Third Man. In effect, Holmes served as a fourth Third Man.

Whenever there was a break in our work schedules—when, say, Hughes would be in the midst of a 24-hour sleep—we would gather in the Third Man bungalow for a poker game. These were dime-ante, quarter-bet affairs that would last only as long as the phone from Hughes didn't ring. During the games the conversation would, inevitably, center on Howard Hughes. We were the only people who had any personal contact with him, and the sessions invariably could have been called "You won't believe it, but . . ." as each of us would recount an incident that happened while in the bungalow with Hughes. We could all do a decent approximation of Hughes's voice, and our recounting of Hughes's battles with Operations were guaranteed to break whatever tension we were feeling.

The Old Man apparently relieved some of his tension by watching movies. But when I got to the hotel I was surprised that the simple act of watching the films didn't give Hughes an even bigger headache than the ones he was escaping from.

There was rich old Howard Hughes, who was renting *five bungalows* at the hotel at $175 a day (one for himself, one for the Major, one for the Third Man crew, and two that Hughes had previously occupied but then moved out of), sitting in a room so cluttered that there was no space between him and the screen for the movies he watched. In fact, the screen was so close to Hughes that when he stretched out in his chair and put his feet out *they were on the other side of the screen.* Another indication of the closeness of the whole business was the fact that the light being projected toward the screen was less than an inch from his head (and his head couldn't have been more than five feet from the screen).

When you project 35-mm movie film a distance of less than 12 feet, what you come up with is a very, very small picture. When you project a Cinemascope or other wide-screen film through a normal projector at that distance, what you get is a moving advertisement for the services of an expert optometrist. (Finally I found it necessary to call an optical company that specialized in movie work and have them grind a lens for Cinemascope projection at that ridiculous range. I never saw the bill for that lens —it must have been extraordinary!—but it worked perfectly, thereby saving the eyes of one rich man and one projectionist.)

I needed my eyesight in that bungalow if only to be able to pick my way through the film cans that were there. Almost every time I went into the bungalow I would take in two film cans that had been delivered by one of the drivers. (A film can is hexagonal—about two feet high and about six to eight inches wide.) Our supply of movies stayed at around 18. With each film in two cans, the 36-can storage problem was horrendous.

Worse than that was trying to return films that just had to be returned. Operations would tell Hughes it was mandatory that a certain film be returned by a certain time. Hughes would always ask them to get an extension. Then he would do his best to forget about it. It was sheer bullheadedness on his part. Many times when he learned that one film was needed by a certain deadline, he'd ask to see different ones. Had we screened that one first, there'd have been no problem. And of course there were occasions when he didn't want to see that film at all: he'd just hold on to it.

I managed to get on his shitlist more than once by trying to be helpful to Operations. I could hear them going back and forth about a film and when it got really bad, I could count on a call from one of the Operations staff. He would tell me about the problem and ask that I sneak the film in question out of the bungalow. I could never convince any of those morons that it was next to impossible to "sneak" out of a bungalow, lugging two large film cans that weighed about 30 pounds each, with Hughes seated less than six feet from the door and me forbidden to leave until he had called the Third Man to get over there and brush the flies away.

Whenever I decided to help Operations by purloining a movie out of the bungalow, I'd simply wait until Hughes made one of his trips to the toilet and then race the cans of film outside and onto the porch. The episode didn't end there, since I also had to rearrange the remaining cans so there wasn't a noticeable gap left by the removal of that particular movie. But the biggest test would always come when Hughes announced that he wanted to see the movie that I had already taken out of the bungalow. It was then that I did *my* Academy-all-the-way performance.

I'd start by looking at all the film cans that remained. Hughes would watch me doing this. I'd get down on my hands and knees and carefully inspect the label on each and every one—and not just once, but several times, until it was painfully obvious that I couldn't find the movie he had asked for.

At that point my ass would be on the line. Hughes knew perfectly well that the movie had been in the room. He knew Operations had been begging him to send it back. He knew there were only two of us in there, and that *he* hadn't been outside in weeks. He knew also that I would never pull a dirty trick on him and that I was giving him my best perplexed look. The circumstantial evidence was against me, and there invariably was an interrogation, which went like this:

"Ron, you don't seem to be able to find the film cans for that movie."

I'd shake my head no.

"Do you want to look again?"

I'd shake my head no.

"Well, it does seem that you have done a thorough job of looking through the remaining cans—but you still seem unable to find it."

I'd nod my head yes.

"You do remember bringing the film into the bungalow; it was, I believe, just two or three days ago?"

I'd nod my head yes.

"Operations has been after me to send that movie back to them for the past several hours, so that would mean that *they* don't have it. But it isn't in the bungalow. Do you have any ideas as to where it might be?"

I'd take out my notepad and write the answer: "No."

"Hmmmm. Would you like to look again to see if you can find it?"

I'd slide off my chair and begin a *very* deliberate and theatrical search for the missing cans. After five or ten minutes, though, I'd come up empty.

"Hmmmm! Ron, you didn't take those cans out by mistake, did you?"

I'd shake my head no.

"Hmmmm! There has not been anyone in this room, other than you or I, for the past twenty-four hours. You didn't take the film cans out, and neither did I. I wonder what happened to them."

I'd reply to that with silence.

We played exactly that game more than once. I assume that Hughes knew what had happened to the film, but we played it out nonetheless. I also assume that Hughes knew that I would only get film out when in my best judgment it was absolutely necessary to do so.

What was getting absolutely necessary for *me* was some sort of resolution to the problem of wetting my whistle when I was on duty in the bungalow. I was expected by Hughes to sit on that birdshit-encrusted chair. (I had within the first days managed to scrape the big pieces off the chair and into the gloomy piles of stuff that littered the floor of the bungalow.) If he wanted movies screened, I screened them. If he didn't, I would sit in silence. Often I would be there for 12 hours straight, or longer, without an opportunity to take a drink of water or go to the toilet. (Not being able to do the former, when you think about it, meant less need to do the latter.)

Water was more important than it might seem, since the bungalow was invariably warmer than it should have been. Hughes refused to turn on either the window-unit air conditioner or the air purifier that sat in another window. The result was that during the warm months in L.A. (and every month usually has a warm spell in it), Bungalow Four had the closeness that you might associate with the monkey house at a zoo during a warm spell

—not the smell, mind you, just that feeling of heaviness in the air.

Hughes had the advantage, in terms of comfort, of his nudity and a supply of water. He would not touch Beverly Hills water from the hotel tap (with cause, I think: Beverly Hills water tastes *awful*). His only drinking water was a commercially bottled concoction from Poland Springs, Maine, packaged under the trade name Poland Water. It was bottled in quart-sized bottles that were dark green, not unlike the color of 7up bottles.

Whenever Hughes got thirsty, if there wasn't some Poland Water around he'd call the Third Man and request a delivery. A few minutes later the Third Man (or Johnnie Holmes) would appear carrying one of the large ice buckets that I had come to hate at Nosseck's. Nestled in ice chips would be a sparkly bottle of Poland Water. (It was obvious that someone had washed the outside of the bottle prior to bringing it to Hughes.)

The delivery would be made by standing in front of Hughes and then extending the bucket and bottle until the top of the bottle was at midchest height for Hughes. The Old Man would then grab some Kleenex and wrap up a bottle opener that sat on the table next to his chair. He'd also take a few sheets of Kleenex and wrap the neck of the bottle. Then he'd remove the cap of the bottle. That was a signal for the bucket to be placed on the floor alongside Hughes's chair. The deliverer would then leave the room. Hughes would then reach down, grab the bottle, and pour some into a glass that he kept on the table. The bottle would stay in the ice bucket when not being used. When Hughes had drunk his way through one bottle, he'd call for another.

It was probably a good thing for Hughes that he was hard of hearing, because he certainly would have been disturbed by the sound of my lips cracking. There seemed to be few possibilities for my getting something to drink. Running a hose from a spigot outside was out. So was the idea of having a plumber run a water line from the porch to the window near my shoulder. So I wrote the Old Man a note: "I have to go to my room for a drink of water."

He took the note, read it, reread it, and then said to me, "Ron, you've only been in the room a short time. Surely you can't be all *that* thirsty. I'm going to let you go to your room very soon and then you can drink all you want. Now go sit down."

Over the next few days, whenever I was called to the bungalow I showed him my note. His reply was always the same: "No." We were in the midst of a hot spell in L.A., and the temperature in that bungalow was pushing 90 degrees. I sat there thinking that while I probably should be happy to have the chance to die of thirst rather than inconvenience Howard Hughes, my death would create a bigger problem for him: the bungalow would fill up with ambulance attendants, police, doctors, all of whom would bring in insects, most of whom would stare at the naked man, and some of whom would wonder how a young man could have died of dehydration in a $175-a-day room, less than six feet from an icy bottle of Poland Water.

Not really wishing to live out my fantasy (literally), I gave Hughes another note. It said, "I am going to *die* of thirst!" That hit a nerve. Hughes stared at me with malice in his eyes.

"Go sit down," he said. He picked up the phone and called the Third Man. "Stan," he said, "Mr. Kistler is thirsty. Mr. Kistler does not have anything to drink. Mr. Kistler reminds me of this fact every two minutes. If I don't get Mr. Kistler something to drink I will never be able to get anything done while he is in the room. Please bring one of *my* bottles of Poland Water to the bungalow so that Mr. Kistler will have something to drink." If someone could have bottled the sarcasm in Hughes's voice he could have sold the venom to the CIA for big bucks.

A few minutes later Stan came in with a bottle of Poland Water sitting in an ice bucket that had no ice. He shoved the bucket at me and left the room. There I was with my very own bottle of Poland Water (of warm Poland Water, to be sure), and, I suddenly realized, no way to open it. Asking Hughes for the use of *his* opener was out of the question. He was sitting in his chair and I could see that his cheeks were flushed with emotion. I found a pair of pliers in the projection equipment and used them to open the bottle. I took a big greedy swallow. It tasted like . . . water. At a buck a quart for Howard Hughes.

That buck was the least of his expenses at the hotel. There were the five bungalows at $175 a day, a room for me at $40 per, and the extraordinary expense of my food. I learned that I was being restricted from a whole range of foods, including pork products, any meat cooked with gravy, garlic, onions, or any other "breath destroyer," spaghetti or any other Italian dish (*my* Italian dish, Virgie, regarded this as another black mark against Hughes), and any food that might be considered exotic. Because the gourmet standards used in measuring what was or wasn't "exotic" were those of that world-renowned center of high-class cuisine—Utah—I found I was safe only with a New York–cut broiled steak. Steak and eggs for breakfast. Steak sandwich for lunch. Steak for dinner. A typical day's food bill for me (You know what room service prices in a good hotel are like today? At the Beverly Hills Hotel the prices were like that *then*.) would run close to $100. The standard Hughes tip was 50 percent of the bill.

I figured that I was costing Hughes around $1300 a week to stay at the hotel and eat that food. Since I was making $464 a week, I considered the budget to be out of balance: I thought I should be getting more than the hotel. Besides, I thought that much money to keep me in food was almost obscene. So I called Operations and got Kay Glenn on the phone. I suggested to him that the prices at the hotel were extremely high and that I would like to make a deal with him. I'd sleep in my station wagon and bring food from home and only charge Operations $500 a week. I'd have done it, but Kay didn't think it was such a hot idea.

"Mr. Hughes wants you to have a room and to take your meals at the hotel," he said frostily. "That is what you will do."

Shot down, I spent some of my time away from the bungalow finding and cultivating the employees who worked in the hotel's room-service department. When they learned that I was up against some Mormons who were trying to make me live up to their dietary standards, they joined me in devising a code so that if I ordered, say, Wheatena and whole-wheat toast with some eggs, what I'd get was ham and eggs. I made up symbols only to cover pork and a few other foods that were obviously taboo to the Mormons. I figured that Hughes had enough to worry about without sniffing out some garlic on my breath.

I knew that he'd smell it on me because he certainly didn't have any on his own breath. His eating habits were better than they had been at Nosseck's, but they were still damned peculiar. He might eat at 8:00 P.M. on a Tuesday and not eat again until 10:00 P.M. on Thursday. He'd call the Third Man and tell him to notify the serving crew that he'd be eating. This call would be placed hours (and sometimes *days*) in advance of his mealtime. Theoretically, this was done so that the service crew could wash themselves and the kitchen down, thereby making everything hygienic for Howard Hughes. In reality, the time between Hughes's call and the service was used by the servers to get back to the hotel from their homes.

Once he called the Third Man and said, "Let's eat steak today." He called back later and said, "I've changed my mind. I'm not going to eat now." It had been two and a half *days* between the first and second calls. This sort of thing wore the waiters to a frazzle. If he ordered steak they would cook it until it was almost done, because they knew that there would be some sort of delay outside the bungalow and they would be standing there with the steak cooking slowly over a Sterno flame. Of course, if the wait outside was too long they would have to go back to the kitchen and start a fresh piece of beef. The record for steaks cooked outside Hughes's bungalow but not delivered inside was, I believe, ten.

Another time it looked as if the waiters were, after innumerable delays, going to get in with their food. They were on the porch with an order of beef stroganoff simmering over the Sterno. Suddenly one of the men looked up at the tile roof of the bungalow. It was evidently the favorite haunt of some sparrows. He reached up with his bare hand and scraped the crusted birdshit off the tiles. He flung it into the stroganoff and then stirred. A short time later the door was opened, the men wheeled the cart inside, and Hughes ate the stroganoff without apparently noticing anything. He didn't say that the meal was better than usual, but he sure didn't say that it was any worse.

However fine his palate might not have been, his ability to pack it away was staggering. A single meal might consist of a large salad, two or three broiled steaks, one or two quarts of milk, several quarts of ice cream, and as many as six single-layer cakes. It would take him two or three hours to finish that amount of food, and I guess it was no wonder that one of them would hold him for days.

Those days were spent working off the meals by sheer dint of nervous energy, which was manifested by Hughes's use of Kleenex. He continually stacked and restacked boxes of Kleenex, as he had at Nosseck's. But he was an ace *using* the individual sheets of the tissue. He used them to wipe his nose, to blow his nose, to dab his nose. To wipe his eyes. To clean out his ears. With the corners twisted, to clean under his fingernails and toenails. He used Kleenex to clean the amplifier of his hearing aid as well as the earpiece. He continually cleaned the telephone, his chair, the ottoman—he cleaned every damned thing he could reach from his chair.

That was peculiar enough. Watching an intelligent man spend two hours wiping the cord that runs from the telephone to the wall is something I recommend for expanding your tolerance of your fellow man. But what that intelligent man *did* after the blowing, dabbing, wiping, and cleaning was calculated to piss anyone off. To dispose of his used Kleenex, Howard Hughes would simply wad up the tissue and throw it over his shoulder onto the floor. Over his shoulder was four feet of space and then *me*. The used Kleenex grew into a healthy pile with each passing day. (Hughes would use from one to two boxes of the stuff a day.)

It grew, as I sat there, until it was about four feet square and three feet high, cone-shaped because there were no natural barriers to build against. I began to fear the possibility of the thing collapsing in my direction, so every time Hughes went into the bathroom for one of his extended attempts to move his bowels, I would spring into action. I moved the line of film cans forward in a line between my chair and his, so that they formed a Maginot Line against the Kleenex. But I was able to move the cans only about an inch at a time, so that Hughes wouldn't notice any radical change in their position. By doing this I thought I could create a wall that would cause any Kleenex collapse to go in *his* direction, not mine.

The longer I sat there, the larger the pile got and the more pissed off I got. I didn't care if Hughes were engulfed in his own dirty tissues. I just didn't want it to happen to me. There were times, in fact, after he had had me there for a day and I was teetering on the brink of exhaustion, when I really believed the damned pile *moved*. I began to see it as a huge jellyfishlike creature that would have made a perfect hero (or is it villain?) in a Japanese sci-fi movie.

Finally Hughes himself began to be concerned with that huge pile of tissues. After I'd been out of the bungalow for a day I noticed that the pile didn't seem as large as it had when I'd left. I didn't think that Hughes would have had some stranger come in there to haul some of it away and I hadn't heard any of the Third Men bitch about having to cart some off, so I figured that what was there had been there when I left. I knew that Hughes wouldn't touch that pile with his hands, so *he* hadn't moved it. I spent almost a week trying to figure out what was happening to the pile, and then one day I spotted the unmistakable outline of a human footprint on the stack. Someone had been stepping on the pile, trying to compress it into a smaller pile. It hadn't been me, and when I questioned the other guys, it hadn't been them.

That left only Howard Hughes. It was something of a relief to know that he would do something about the pile, but then he went further. On occasion when I came back to the bungalow after a day off, or even after a few hours, I'd notice that *someone* had moved that row of film cans toward *my* chair. It turned out that two could play that little game, and two did.

Chapter 13

The idea that Howard Hughes and I were jockeying film cans back and forth to form a barrier against a mini-mountain of dirty Kleenex is absurd, but no more so than the realization that he sat nude in that room and wrestled (in his own way) with one of the more dramatic problems of American business. Hughes was pulling out all the stops to raise cash for the purchase of the jetliners for TWA.

On the one hand he was directing the negotiations that were taking place between the lending agencies and his attorneys. But he was also trying to get rid of various assets that would bring in some cash. He even went so far as to call a broker specializing in aircraft sales and offer for sale the Convair 440 and DC-6 I had been guarding at the airport. The sale never materialized, but during Hughes's phone conversations I finally learned the reason behind the 24-hour-a-day guard that had been put on the planes. The broker had wanted to know why the planes were guarded, and Hughes replied that he had a sport coat hanging in the Convair that had $17,000 in cash in one of the pockets. (While I had been on that guard detail I had often idly speculated on what it cost to keep that area secure and calculated that it ran to about $30,000 a year.)

But Hughes increasingly turned his attentions to squeezing some money out of the Howard Hughes Medical Institute, which had its headquarters in Miami, Florida. HHMI got its money from Hughes Aircraft, a situation resulting from a scientists' revolt at Hughes Aircraft a few years earlier. The U.S. Air Force, which supplied most of the contracts that made Hughes Aircraft profitable, had threatened to withdraw its support if the company wasn't made stable. Well, stability in that case meant keeping Hughes's hands off the management of the company. So Hughes set up a nonprofit organization, HHMI, which owned the aircraft company. But the sole trustee for HHMI was Howard Hughes. Furthermore, the land and buildings occupied by the aircraft company were owned by Hughes Tool. It seemed to Hughes that somewhere in that arrangement there existed the possibility of getting some money out of the profitable aircraft company or HHMI.

His first tactic was to take a long look at the HHMI bank account, which contained $18 million. He called one of his attorneys, a man in New York City, and instructed him to find a way to get that money away from HHMI and into the accounts of the tool company. The attorney tried to dissuade Hughes, reminding him that the government regulations in effect for nonprofit institutions such as HHMI expressly forbade such a plan.

Hughes was frantic and made no attempt to hide his feelings. "I know," he blurted into the phone, "that it isn't possible without a great amount of effort. But I want you to review the entire structure of the Institute and find *some* way to get that money out of there."

A couple of days later he received a call-back message

from the attorney, and, on returning the call, was informed that it was impossible to touch that money by any means. I figured that was that. But Hughes sat and played with his Kleenex boxes for a couple of days and then called the attorney back.

"I've accepted your opinion," Hughes said, "that we cannot get the money out of the Institute. But I do have another plan that I want you to put into effect immediately. Since Toolco [the corporate abbreviation for Hughes Tool Company] owns the land and the leasehold improvements at Hughes Aircraft, we should have some latitude in the lease agreement. I want you to figure out the mechanics that would enable Hughes Aircraft to prepay its lease fees. The timespan should be calculated to assure that the amount would be eighteen. [Hughes never bothered to add the "million" after a number. When he said "six," he meant "six million."] Then we can have that amount released to Toolco."

It sounded beautifully simple. The right hand would take care of the left, and in the end TWA would get delivery of more of its jet fleet. I wasn't surprised to hear the attorney gasping as Hughes proposed his scheme. The next day Hughes called the attorney again. He wanted to know *when*—not if—the money would be available. He was so positive that I hardly expected the lawyer to say that the plan wasn't possible. But that's what happened. The attorney had a number of reasons why the idea was not only unworkable but also illegal. Hughes fought him on every word. He countered every argument with his own interpretation. It was magnificent. The attorney was citing all the legal ramifications and applicable laws, while Hughes was in effect saying that the whole thing was insane. He owned Toolco, he owned 78 percent of TWA, he was the sole trustee for HHMI, which owned Hughes Aircraft, and so it was a simple matter of taking funds out of one pocket and putting them into another. In a gentle voice at the end of the call, he told the lawyer just to do what Howard Hughes wanted done and not make any waves as he did it. Then Hughes hung up.

The next time they spoke the attorney calmly told Hughes that what he wanted done was simply impossible. He also said that he would not consider any more requests of that sort and that if Hughes didn't like it, Hughes could just get himself another attorney. Then the attorney hung up. It took Hughes a couple of days to calm down enough to call the man back, but when he did, it was to say that the man should proceed with the negotiations to borrow the money TWA needed. The plan to get money out of HHMI was dead.

All of this business was being done by phone. There were rare occasions when I or another employee would hand-carry messages, but the bulk of Hughes's transactions were by telephone. Hughes was managing this with one simple desk-model phone, a single line with no hold buttons or frills.

Hughes would call Operations frequently to check on his incoming calls. Most of the messages left for him were ignored. Some were acknowledged only by telling Operations to handle them according to some long-established procedure or other. The messages that Hughes considered important enough for his personal attention were handled in one of two ways. First, the entire message was read to him: the time of the call, the name of the staff member who had handled it, the name of the party, and the entire conversation—including vocal inflections, pauses, stammers, sighs, laughs, or any other mannerisms that might indicate the state of mind of the caller. On many occasions these messages would be read and reread to Hughes, often as many as five times, before the Old Man was satisfied that he had the correct interpretation of the call. If he felt that Operations could safely handle the action necessitated by the call, Hughes let them do it. He would dictate to a staff man the entire message he wanted relayed. The man would be cautioned to relay the message exactly as Hughes gave it. Often the staff man would have to repeat the message to Hughes so that the Old Man could edit or correct the presentation. It might take three or four trial runs before Hughes was satisfied. After the return calls had been placed by Operations, Hughes would be informed of the call and what response, if any, there had been on the part of the person receiving the call.

A very few phone calls were personally handled by Hughes. He would get the phone number of the other party from Operations and then go through a drill to make certain he had the message and frame of mind of the caller down pat. He'd have the staff man run through that call a number of times (except for the phone number —Hughes would memorize those after hearing them once). Sometimes he would tell Operations to call the other party to alert them that Hughes himself would be calling them at a certain time and to ask that they make themselves available for the call. Other times he would simply dial the number when it was convenient for him to do so. Sometimes, of course, he'd change his mind about returning a call. If Operations had alerted the person who was supposed to get the call, he would be sitting there waiting for a phone to ring. The disappointment of these people would be evidenced by their subsequent calls to Operations to find out what had gone wrong. (The president of TWA, Charlie Thomas, was the most frequent victim of Hughes deciding not to call back after Operations had said he would.)

The rarest kind of call was an incoming call to Hughes's bungalow. If someone were given the number, it was only because Hughes had authorized it and wanted very much to speak to that person. The incoming calls were always scheduled through Operations, so that someone wouldn't call when Hughes was unavailable. Most of the people who were allowed to call in were in a position to do Hughes some good.

The Old Man could be the most charming guy in the world when he wanted to, and he generally turned it on when he got an incoming call. (Some of the calls, though, were from people who had crossed him in some way or had to report bad news. You just can't imagine what a good ass-chewing is until you've heard Howard Hughes deliver one. He is not given to obscenity in his normal speech—he's soft-spoken and very much a gentleman. But when he got pissed off at someone he'd demonstrate total recall of the language he learned in the Texas oil fields. I heard some very powerful, aggressive, belligerent callers turned into semimutes by Hughes.)

I was privy to these calls because of Hughes's hearing problem. He was forced to wear a hearing aid, so he did not hold the telephone in a normal manner. He reversed it, holding the earpiece to the amplifier of the hearing device and the mouthpiece in front of his mouth. I could hear both sides of the conversation from where I sat, and Hughes knew it. Whenever there was something he didn't want me to hear, he'd send me to my room. But most of the time I stayed, and more than once Hughes asked me, after he had completed the call, to recall for him something that had been said or *how* it had been put. He asked me not to allow anything I heard to leave the room, which caused me no end of problems with the staff at Operations. *They* were most anxious to know what was going on, and they would pump me for information, which I simply wouldn't supply. It was indicative of how things were in the Hughes empire that the only people who tried to make me reveal what was going on with Hughes himself were the people who worked for him.

That was understandable. Knowledge is, after all, power, and the people at Operations would be stripped of some of their power if they didn't know what was really happening with the man they were supposed to be serving. I recall one incoming call to Hughes that Operations had arranged in advance. It was so clearly a matter of delicacy that I knew something big was in the works, and I figured that I was going to be sent to my room. In fact, I looked forward to being sent to my room so that I could shower and have some time to myself. But as the scheduled time approached for the incoming call, I was dismayed to find that I was being allowed to stay in the bungalow. At the precise moment for which the call was scheduled, the phone rang.

A voice I had never heard before identified himself as a "Major Hughes" of Washington, D.C. (It was probably a prearranged code name. Using bogus code names on the phone was standard Hughes procedure.) After a few normal social amenities the two men got to the meat of the conversation. Major Hughes was calling to conclude the arrangements for air travel, limousine transportation, hotel accommodations, meals, and entertainment for a large number of influential guests who would be traveling from Washington, D.C., to the Los Angeles area. They were obviously all coming for a function.

It seemed that Howard Hughes was the sole sponsor of the trip; and if I interpreted his mood correctly, he was pleased to have the opportunity to play host. Major Hughes supplied the Old Man with a head count, the preferences of several guests as to transportation and hotels, and other requirements of the VIPs who would be coming. Howard Hughes was so completely charming that it was difficult to believe a naked, scraggly-haired millionaire hidden in a darkened bungalow could be uttering the words he uttered. When all of the details had been confirmed, Howard Hughes closed the conversation by saying, "It's nice to talk with you again. I'm glad I can be of help. Give my regards to your man. Please call if I can be of any further help."

Shortly after this call, and after Hughes had relayed the instructions to Operations, I was allowed to go to my room. Hughes hadn't slept for a couple of days, so I knew I could count on him to sleep for at least a full day, and perhaps two. I made my arrangements with the Third Man and went home to visit my family. (The Third Man was vital to these unauthorized leaves. When Hughes called and told him to get me over to the bungalow, he had to know how to get in contact with me immediately. I could get back to the hotel within about 25 minutes—I never left my home when I was AWOL from the hotel—and if I got caught in traffic and got chewed out by Hughes for being delayed, I'd resort to the perfect alibi: I'd apologize but say that I had been having a bowel movement. That was one thing that Hughes held in almost religious awe. I could have beat a murder rap by telling the jury that I killed a guy because he interrupted my bowel movement—if the jury had been made up of twelve Howard Hugheses.)

On this occasion I finished my visit and got back to the hotel to find that Hughes was still conked out. As I watched the late news on television I was interested to see a news story from Los Angeles International Airport. The film showed a TWA plane taxiing up to the terminal. A red carpet was rolled out and a horde of newsmen rushed to the ramp. The doors of the plane opened, and a most impressive parade of senators, congressmen, cabinet members, and, if my eyes didn't deceive me, a Supreme Court justice or two deplaned. The film went on to show this blue-ribbon group going through the terminal and getting into a fleet of limousines.

The purpose of their visit was a gala occasion for the Republican Party. The fine citizens of Whittier, California, had decided to pay homage to their most illustrious son—then Vice-President Richard M. Nixon. Now, you know and I know that if no one shows up at one of these functions except some townies and some local pols, it means a massive loss of prestige. On the other hand, to turn out some heavy hitters is a boost to the person being honored. Someone had done his homework very well in this case. The affair was well-covered by the media, even though the name of the mystery host was never mentioned.

That such an event was organized by phone was not only a tribute to Hughes's sense of the ways things should be done and his passion for privacy, but also to his trust in the man who swept his phone line for bugs. He had a morbid fear that someone might successfully tap his line, so the technician would come in frequently to check the line. The phone number was changed often to make bugging more difficult. Anyone who thought he could learn about Hughes by tapping one of his subordinates' phones would have been out of luck, too. Whenever one of these people had something important to discuss with the Old Man, he would go to an out of the way phone booth and call him from there. That procedure was a firm rule. He'd check it by asking for the number and calling it right back. That not only ensured that the person was in a phone booth and not at home (Hughes had memorized the home number in most cases and also knew which numbers differed markedly either in exchange or in other numbers from those reserved for pay phones), but also allowed the conversation to proceed without fear of interruption from an operator looking for more money.

There were times when I felt like *I* was interrupting something—when the Old Man was talking on the phone with either the Major or the Party. I was extremely embarrassed when he talked with his wife, a woman I had come to like at Goldwyn. I would sit there, listening to all of the man-woman, husband-wife intimacies, the spats, the gossip, the problems, and so on. I tried to indicate to Hughes that I was uncomfortable listening to these calls, but he would ramble on for hours on end.

Much of the time he was telling her the kinds of things a married couple living a more normal life would have out over a drink at the end of the working day. Hughes informed her about the TWA crisis and complained that if he didn't get it resolved soon he was afraid it was going to drive him batty. As soon as it was resolved, he once said to her, he wanted her to book the two of them on a world cruise, or for a vacation to wherever she wanted to go, and he'd take off for a year with her. He also made promises to her regarding housing, as I mentioned earlier. There he would be in *his* hotel bungalow, talking on the phone to his wife, who was about 50 yards away in *her* hotel bungalow, discussing whether they should buy or build and where she would like to live, and so on.

If it was difficult to understand why the Old Man chose to live the way he did, it was equally hard to figure out why the Major put up with what could only be described as a very unorthodox life-style. She was a Phi Beta Kappa from a Midwestern university and a woman of a quick and lively mind who was willingly enduring a life of extreme isolation. She went from hobby to hobby—ceramics, needlepoint, welding sculpture out of metal—while Hughes wouldn't allow her to go out and do the things she wanted to do. She loved baseball, and the Dodgers had just come to L.A., but Hughes wouldn't allow her to go to the Coliseum. If she wanted to go out shopping, she'd make it one time out of ten.

Hughes wouldn't turn her down flat. He was too much the diplomat for that. He'd tell her, honey, I know you want to go and I *want* you to go, but I don't want you to go just yet, I want you to wait awhile. Or he would use the white-glove detail—they were the drivers for the Major—to delay or postpone her trips. One of his outs if she wanted to go shopping was to call Operations and tell them to set it up with her. But when it was time for the car to arrive to pick her up, he had a staff member call her and say that the driver had come down with a severe attack of influenza and that the trip would have to wait. I think she was too smart not to see what was happening, and perhaps one of the reasons she kept dreaming up things to do was to see how he'd get out of allowing her to do them. After all, every time you use up one alibi, you have to come up with a new one.

At least the Major accepted Hughes's alibis or explanations or evasions—all the things he did that not only kept them separate, but also kept her away from other people. The Party, that special starlet who had been given an Imperial convertible and lived in a new, expensive house about five miles above the hotel in Coldwater Canyon, was much less understanding. She had maid service, pool service, garbage service, her every need was cared for, and she got a better salary than the other starlets, but she didn't appear to have much talent. She was young, and she didn't care to be cooped up, no matter how nice the house. Whenever Hughes called her, she'd really let him have it. She didn't want to be in that sonofabitchin' house, she wanted *out*. If he said that it was a nice day, she'd immediately find a cloud outside. I don't know why he put up with it, but we were supposed to cater to her.

If Hughes got any respite from the Party and the TWA matter and whatever else was bothering him at the time, he got it from the movies we screened and a couple of trips he made out of the bungalow. Apparently, these were some of the last trips he made before settling into the cocoon he has remained in to this day.

He had committed himself, Toolco, and TWA to Lockheed Aircraft to purchase some interim aircraft that were supposed to serve in the period between the propeller planes and the pure jets: the prop-jet Lockheed Electras. When the airplanes rolled off the assembly lines, Hughes wanted to try one out. I had heard some of the preparations being made over the phone, but something had always come up to delay the trip. Finally, on a bright Sunday morning, Hughes was ready to go. I was to be involved.

The plan was for Hughes to go from the bungalow, turn left (east) and leg it for Crescent Drive, where Johnnie Holmes had the car. It was a distance of about 50 yards. The plan (which was treated with as much seriousness as the plan for D-Day) was to ensure that Hughes could travel those 50 yards without being seen or heard *or* served with one of several subpoenas that had his name on it.

My job on this detail was to stand behind a palm tree that bordered the sidewalk, about midway between the hotel and the car. One of the Third Man detail stood behind another tree on the other side of the walk, slightly closer to the street. Johnnie Holmes stood beside the car, with the right rear door open. The door to the bungalow would be opened by one of the Third Men. He would follow Hughes to the car, protecting the rear flank. Hughes squeezed out of the bungalow door at the appropriate moment, headed down the steps, through the patio, and followed the sidewalk to the car. His pace was something of a trot, and as he went he kept turning his head from side to side to make sure that someone didn't sneak up on him. If someone *had* it would have provided a very interesting moment, since none of us had been told by Operations what we could (or should) do in such a case. The should part of it was assumed to be to keep people away from the Old Man. But that assumption fell apart when we tried to guess how far we could go in performing our jobs. If, for example, a man had started walking up Crescent Drive on the public sidewalk just as Hughes started out of the bungalow and if I had walked up to the presumed civilian and asked him to freeze and if he had decided not to comply, what was I to do? Any physical act on my part would have either got me in a fight or arrested, or both. Would Operations bail me out? I didn't know. No one did. Fortunately there was no incident on the two trips that Hughes made to Lockheed.

He certainly had no problems when he got to the Lockheed plant. The guards at the gates had been notified that he was coming and simply waved our cars through without our even having to slow down. Because we were arriving on a Sunday morning there was a skeleton crew at the Burbank plant, and the workers seemed to have been given orders to keep a respectable distance from our group.

Hughes was met by a couple of distinguished-looking men—without, however, the polite formality of a handshake—and ushered up the steps of a loading ramp and into a shiny new Electra. The plane taxied onto the landing strip and a short time later flew off. I got out of the back-up car and sat on the fender, hoping that Hughes wasn't going to pull one of his famous disappearing acts. He had previously tested one of the Lockheed Constellations, taking it East for months, while the wives of the crew and the executives of TWA—which was waiting for delivery of the plane—fumed.

A few minutes after the plane took off I saw it coming back on an approach pattern. I thought it was strange that Hughes would have kept it up for such a short time. But as I watched, the plane landed without stopping, revved up, and took off again. The Electra made a slow circle around the airport and repeated that procedure— landing without stopping and taking off again. I asked a passing Lockheed worker what the hell that was all about, and he told me that it's called "shooting touch and go's" and tests a plane's power and response to emergency situations, among other things. Hughes put the craft through about 12 touch and go's.

While Hughes was buzzing around the airstrip I was joined by a man in flight coveralls who had come out of one of the hangars. He looked as if he had just come from one of the planes that lined the runways. He watched the Electra shoot three or four touch and go's and then turned to me and said, "That must be Howard Hughes flying that plane. He's the only man I know who can handle a plane that perfectly." The name on the guy's coveralls was Fish Salmon. Later I learned he was one of the ace test pilots at Lockheed.

He wandered off and a short time later Hughes landed the plane and pulled over to the place he had started from. The ramp was wheeled out and Hughes emerged from the plane. He got back into his car and we all headed back to the hotel. The elapsed time of the outing was less than four hours. (I heard that Hughes also test flew the Boeing 707, which must have raised a few eyebrows since the Old Man hadn't been licensed to fly jets.)

Getting out to fly was a rare bit of fun for Hughes. His support troops at the hotel had to contrive their own. None of the waiters or Third Men were Mormons, which is important to remember when you consider the fun they had with the smoking routine. The first thing they had discovered was that the air purifier that sat unused in one of Hughes's windows was near enough to my shoulders that I could hear through its screening. (Hughes, with his hearing problem, couldn't.) During those times when the waiters were outside, standing around in expectation of being summoned inside, they would whisper jokes through the purifier, hoping to break me up. Soon, however, they discovered that smoke could pass through the purifier as easily as jokes.

They knew that I smoked and that I wasn't allowed to when I was in with the Old Man. Since *they* all smoked, they knew I was dying for a cigarette. They decided to oblige me. Nice guys. I'd be sitting there smelling tobacco and salivating for one of my Viceroys. Finally they began to escalate their smoke-blowing, so much so that Hughes began sniffing the air.

"Ron," he said, "I smell smoke. Are you smoking?"

I nodded no.

"Well, I smell smoke."

I nodded yes.

"I smell smoke and *I'm* not smoking. *You're* not smoking. But I *do* smell smoke. Do *you* smell smoke?"

I nodded yes.

"Isn't that strange? That's the first time I've ever smelled smoke here."

While this was going on, the guys outside were lighting up one after another and blowing smoke through that damned purifier.

"Ron, I know you smoke—I've seen you with cigarettes. But you're not smoking now. I asked you and you said you weren't smoking."

I nodded no.

"But I do *smell* smoke and *you* smell smoke. Isn't it strange?"

What was really strange was that Hughes apparently couldn't hear the howls of laughter from outside. My revenge would come when they came inside. The waiters and the Third Man and Johnnie Holmes would all have to serve Hughes facing him, which meant that they were also facing *me*. So I began to try and break them up behind Hughes's back. They'd be concentrating on getting his delivery of Poland Water or food or newspapers or magazines just right and I'd stand up quietly, turn my back, and do a few bars of "Shine On, Harvest Moon," by pulling down my pants and showing them my Limoges-like buttocks. If they started laughing when Hughes was doing something very important and serious, like concentrating on getting the middle newspaper out of the pile of three, he'd almost take it as a personal affront. So he'd turn around and look to see what the hell *I* was doing. I would be playing Buster Keaton back there. It's hard to believe he didn't know what was going on. I suspect that he did but that he knew it was our way of blowing off steam. Maybe he appreciated that it was at his expense because he was the one who was creating all the tension to begin with.

He did have another outing that helped *him* to relax. It happened at the end of December 1958. In fact, you can say that December 24th was a red-letter day in Hughes's life. First, it was his 52nd birthday. Because it was his birthday he had found a way, as was his custom, to have all of his buddies at the hotel. There were a great number of people running around on contrived errands. Almost as good as his birthday, though, was the fact that there was a brushfire raging in Benedict Canyon, another of the ultrarich hillsides above Beverly Hills. I don't mean to imply that Hughes was turned on by fire or by tragedy. But this one delighted him, because the home of Noah Dietrich, his former right-hand man, lay in the path of the fire. I had spent the day in the bungalow, and I heard Hughes stay in close contact with Operations. He was getting up-to-the-minute reports on the progress of the fire, and as it moved closer to the Dietrich address, Hughes's interest grew. I began to wonder if he would break down and turn on the TV, since L.A. television stations are noted for live coverage of local disasters. But he didn't. (Not then, not *ever* while I was in the bungalow.)

Perhaps he was holding himself together for date night. That was the capper to the whole day. I'd heard all of the preparations being made, and it sounded like a prom was being held at Bungalow Four. The Party had been invited to come down from her house and be the guest of Howard Hughes at Bungalow Six. (Bungalow Six was one of the empties that Hughes kept paying for.) The rendezvous was scheduled for 10:00 P.M.

As evening fell I was allowed to leave the bungalow.

Hughes had eaten and allowed the waiters and Third Men to go to their quarters. (All three Third Men had been told to stay at the hotel.) Johnnie Holmes had been called to the hotel and was waiting in the Third Man bungalow, number One. The inevitable poker game started in Bungalow One, and we all were telling our "You won't believe it . . ." stories. After a few hours the game petered out, and we started looking for other ways to stay amused. (We wanted to stay *very* amused and therefore forget that it was Christmas Eve and that we wanted to be home with our families.)

I suggested we go on the roof of the new wing of the hotel and watch the fire. About four of us left Bungalow One and went up to the roof, where we were rewarded with a spectacular view of the out-of-control flames shooting up from the canyon. As we stood there we also had an excellent view of the grounds of the Beverly Hills Hotel. There was Bungalow Four, and right over *there* was Bungalow Six. Just before 10:00 P.M. we saw a familiar blue Imperial convertible pull up to the curb on Crescent Drive. The Party got out and quickly made her way to Bungalow Six. A short time later the door opened at Bungalow Four. There was no one there to brush the flies away. There was no one there to guard Hughes. The Old Man let himself out and headed for Bungalow Six. He had dressed up for the occasion. A pair of slacks, tan in color and too large in size, complemented his white shirt. It had been freshly laundered, and even if it was much too large, it was open at the neck to give the man breathing room. The same old brown wing-tips were on his feet, although we were too far away and it was too dark to see if he'd gone all the way and found himself laces and a pair of socks. Still, the man was all duded up.

As he trotted from Bungalow Four to Bungalow Six we

kept looking from one side to the other, just as he had when he went out to his car. It took him less than 30 seconds to cover the distance between the two buildings. I saw a flash of Kleenex in his hand as he opened the door and disappeared into number six.

We continued to stand on the roof, watching the fire, and out of the corners of our eyes, number six. Suddenly a familiar figure appeared on the walkway. It was Johnnie Holmes, headed for Bungalow Six. He was carrying a small service tray covered with a pink napkin. Naturally, we had to holler down at Holmes to make sure he was aware of our seeing him and to make certain he followed all regulations. He looked up in the dim light from the sidewalk lamps and gave us what I interpreted as a sour look. When he got to number six he took a piece of Kleenex out of his pocket, opened the door, and went inside. He came out a few seconds later, flipped us the finger, and went back toward Bungalow One. A few minutes later one of the guys who had stayed in number one joined us on the roof to report. Holmes had delivered two daiquiris to Bungalow Six and had been told to return to One and wait for further instructions.

The fire was still raging on the skyline above the hotel, but we got bored watching it and went back to One to try to occupy ourselves. Just as we got there Hughes called Holmes and asked him to bring two more daiquiris to Six. When Holmes got back he told us to expect the worst—Hughes and the Party seemed to be having a wonderful time and we were all expected to spend Christmas Day at the fabulous Beverly Hills Hotel.

I went back to my room and called home to make certain that Santa Claus had made it to our house. Virgie told me that the kids were going to get a lot of nice presents but that they weren't going to have a nice

Christmas. The reason, of course, was Howard Hughes. He was going to ruin a family day. She really lit into me, and after the call was over I turned to the companionship of a bottle of Old Hickory bourbon. After a time I decided that Howard Hughes and Santa Claus had only one thing in common: long hair and a long beard.

It was early morning, Christmas Day, and I hadn't been able to sleep, so I was walking around. I headed out to Crescent Drive and noticed that the Imperial convertible was gone. I walked past Bungalow Six. It was dark. I walked around Bungalow Four. It was dark. I went down to the hotel garage, got into my car, and headed for my house in Van Nuys. I was going to spend at least part of Christmas with my family whether Howard Hughes liked it or not.

I spent a wonderful day with my family. The only anxious moments came when the phone rang. Happily, none of the calls were from the hotel. It was about midnight when I went back. I went to Bungalow One and wasn't really surprised to find that everyone else had gone home, the same as I had. The only guy there was one of the Third Men, and he had spent part of the day at his home.

We needn't have worried about being caught by Hughes. It was three full days before any of us heard from him. We did hear, in those three days, from Operations, which wanted to know what the *dickens* was going on and where was Mr. *Hughes,* for gosh sakes. I don't know what happened in Bungalow Six, but at the time I was all for repeat performances that would get me off the hook for three days. The only dark spot, if you could call it that, was that the fire had been stopped before it could burn Dietrich out. Hughes wasn't happy with that news.

I don't know how he would have reacted to the fact

that I had begun to spend a lot of my off-duty time in the bar at the hotel. There were many days when I wasn't called into the bungalow. I'd read paperbacks or watch TV, but when I got bored I'd head for the Polo Lounge. It was only the hotel bar to me, but in the world of show business it's one of the key places in L.A. to do business, make deals, or be seen. I'd shoot the shit with the bartender or any other soul I could corner. Actually, I shared drinks with some fairly well-known people, not because of my engaging personality but because, I think, the word went out that I worked for Hughes. No question was too personal to be asked about the man: Who was he laying, how often, did the women enjoy it? Yet no one *ever* asked me directly if I really worked for Hughes. All their questions went unanswered, partly because it was none of their business, partly because I'd been coached to shut up.

And, perhaps, partly because I never got to spend a great deal of time in the Polo Lounge. I always figured that a lot of the people working at the hotel were being paid by Operations. I knew I'd been fingered as being at the bar when I saw a waiter coming my way with a telephone. The messages never varied, only the degree of alarm in the voice of the caller.

"Now, Ron, you *know* that you are not allowed to drink alcoholic beverages when you are associated with Mr. Hughes. We want you to go back to your room and stay there." *Click!* They wouldn't even give me time for a witty response. Most of the time I'd finish my drink and head on back to my room. Other times I'd head past the liquor store and pick up a fifth. But the real fun came when I would be bullheaded and stay in the bar. I might be in the middle of a discussion about something really important—sports—and simply not want to leave. It would take around 30 or 45 minutes before Operations could muster the troops. If one of my good friends was at the drivers' room, he'd draw the assignment. Operations would tell him to go to the hotel, proceed immediately to the bar, and get me to my room. If it were one of my friends, he'd sit down with me, have a drink or two for himself, and then suggest that we call it a day. Not wishing to get a pal in trouble, I'd always heed his advice. He could then go back to the drivers' room and report success.

If Operations sent someone I *didn't* like, I'd just ignore him until he left. When I did that I had to be prepared to deal with one of the high and mighty staff members. Most of them were good Mormons, and about as out of place in a bar as a belly dancer at a ballet. They were never loud. Their pleas were always delivered in a monotone: "Ron, you've got to go back to your room. You know that you are wrong in being here, and if Mr. Hughes finds out you're going to be in bad trouble. Now, please, go back to your room." I always waited for the word "please." Then I'd drain my drink in one gulp while he was watching me. (There is something comical about the look on a good Mormon's face when he watches you poison yourself.)

I had always been suspicious about the no-drinks rule, and after I found out that Hughes himself had had a nip, I felt it was okay for me to do so. I decided to put my theory to a great test on January 31, 1959. It was my birthday, and the workload leading up to it had convinced me that Hughes would be out of circulation for at least 24 hours. Since I wasn't going to race over the mountains, I went to the liquor store and picked up two quarts of 100-proof vodka and went back to my room, prepared to be left breathless. I called Operations and had them tell room service to send me a healthy quart of freshly squeezed orange juice and a bucket of ice cubes. Then I called the drivers' room and left word for my two best buddies—Bill Brimley was one—that they were needed at my room at the hotel. I only had time for three or four screwdrivers before the first of my friends joined me. When I told him what the celebration was about, he was only too happy to join in. We had a sizable headstart when Brimley finally showed up at 4:00 P.M.

Within an hour the vodka had disappeared, so we decided to join the cocktail hour of the real world, already in progress in the Polo Lounge. We enjoyed about an hour there before the phone was handed to me. It was a staff man, and I thought he must somehow have been drinking, because I couldn't make any sense of the conversation. My buddies and I decided that it would probably be a good thing if we left, so we got a car and left the hotel. Many, many bars and many, many hours later we finally decided that we should call it a night. By then we were in downtown L.A., and it was questionable whether any of us could walk, let alone drive. Somehow, though, we got back to the hotel. As we staggered into my room we were surprised to find a Hughes driver, Norm, sitting there waiting for us.

Norm gave us a quick rundown. Hughes had called for me just after we left the Polo Lounge. He wanted me to bring two cans of film into the bungalow. He had been calling the Third Man at half-hour intervals wanting to know what the hell was holding me up. Operations had been notified early in the evening, and they had started a massive manhunt. When it became known that my two friends were with me, all the off-duty drivers were called in, our closest friends were questioned, our wives were called, repeatedly, and men were sent to our known watering holes. All of this was to no avail because we had gone to a section of town that was new to us. Norm left the room after telling us all this and reappeared a few moments later with a huge pot of hot coffee. I drank several cups and found to my amazement that the coffee was pushing the alcohol out of my stomach and into my brain. I was totally, completely, utterly, thoroughly, sensationally drunk. It was obvious to everyone that I would need around 24 hours to get myself together. It was also obvious, perhaps only to me, that I should deliver the film cans to Hughes, *right then*.

It seemed so *clear*. That would get Hughes off my back and would allow me to return to my room and get some sleep. It was rather chilly out, so I put on a heavy, lined car-coat and went to the bungalow. I met the Third Man at Bungalow Four and picked up the two film cans. After he had waved his newspaper at the sleeping (or incubating) insects, I made my grand entrance. The room must have been 85 degrees. (Hughes's only clothing, the hotel napkin, measured 21 by 19½ inches. In the world of napkins it is a grand object, bright pink with the hotel crest in its middle. In the world of clothing it is not what you'd wear in the winter, even in California.)

As I came face to face with Hughes I had a great inspiration. I would give him my best, my most disarming, my most magnificent, smile. It would say, "Hi, there, ain't I somethin', a good ol' country boy." After I put it on my face I looked at Hughes. No effect.

"Ron, stand right where you're at."

I stood as stolidly as I could, but I imagine that I was beginning to wobble. The film cans, which weighed about 40 pounds each, had thin metal handles that seemed to have been honed to razor sharpness. I began to have visions of being a drunken amputee. I began to feel as if I were going to pass out from the heat. I stood there for what seemed like hours while Hughes looked around for a place to put those cans.

Finally he said, "Just set the cans over by your chair and come back here and stand in that spot." I had to pry my fingers off the handles, then I staggered back to the place where I was to stand. My only hope was that I wouldn't pass out and hit Hughes on the way down.

He began to smile. "Have you had quite enough to drink tonight, Ron?"

This time I *couldn't* open my mouth to speak. I nodded yes. Hughes began to laugh the special low-key laugh he reserved for a few occasions.

"Go to your room and sleep it off," he said. "I won't call you for a couple of days." Then he began to guffaw as I staggered out the door.

I managed to get past the porch steps and into some convenient foliage before I puked. The bungalow smelled like a brewery for a couple of days, but Hughes never mentioned my behavior again.

Chapter 14

Practically speaking, one of the reasons Hughes wasn't about to carry on about my one-time drunk was that he knew it was letting off steam and also because I was acting above and beyond the call with regard to the Party. The night of the rainstorm was one example.

It had been pouring, a torrential storm, since noon. At around 10:00 in the evening I had been sent back to my room after a couple of days of long sessions in the bungalow. I was whipped, and Hughes had been fairly nasty —short, abrupt, caustic. Room service had appeared with the first food I had had time to eat in over a day. I was looking forward to a hot shower and a chance to remove a three-day growth of beard. Just as I was heading for the bathroom the phone rang. It was Hughes himself. That was enough to get my adrenalin up, since he usually called for me through the Third Man.

"Ron, get over here immediately." Click. I ran off about 25 of my best obscenities into the phone.

It was about 35 yards from my building to the bungalow. I ran out with my car-coat over my head into a small cascade of water. It had gotten a lot worse in the time I'd been inside. The hills of Beverly had soaked up about as much as they could hold, and everything that was coming down was also coming down slope, trying to get to a level area or storm sewer, whichever came first. I sloshed my way to Hughes's patio and looked around for the Third Man to open the door and sweep away the flies. One look in the direction of the Third Man bungalow told me that there wouldn't be a Third Man to do his job. Bungalow One was downstream of a small river that was sweeping cushions from patio furniture and other assorted debris through the grounds. Finally, with water pouring off the roof and onto me, I acted out of desperation, opening the door and going into the bungalow.

Several things happened that distracted Hughes, so that he overlooked the breach of rules regarding entry procedure. The first was a four-inch wave of water entering the room when I did. (Hughes's patio resembled a wading pool.) Then there was me, with water pouring off my coat and arms.

Hughes looked at me, and then, in a sarcastic tone, gave me my instructions. "Go sit in your chair," he said.

I went and sat in my chair. Hughes sat in his chair, and there we were for the next two hours. Everything I had on was soaked through. My teeth began to chatter, and when they did Hughes peered around the corner of his chair and gave me a look that I'm certain was supposed to terrify me into cutting out my silly behavior. He got really steamed whenever my body would begin to shiver uncontrollably.

Finally I learned *why* Hughes wanted me back there. He picked up the phone and made a call, and it became evident that he had been warned by Operations that it was a call he would have to make. He called the Party, because she was having a tantrum.

After three or four rings I heard a woman's voice.

177

There is no point in reproducing the profanity she used in its entirety. Anyone who has been in the armed services or dropped a hot iron on his or her hand knows all the forms of the word "fuck," as well as the longer words celebrating mom and quaint sex acts.

"You tell those double-bleeping bleeps in Operations that when I call and tell them to do something I want it done that same bleeping instant!"

"Well, honey—" Hughes began.

"Don't honey me, you old bastard. I'm sick and tired of being a bleeping prisoner in this bleeping house and I'm leaving!" That was her ultimate threat.

"I can tell that you are upset—"

"You bet your sweet ass I'm upset. The bleeping maid didn't come today, there's dogshit all over the house, the bleeping electricity was off for four hours, and I'm hungry."

"I'm sorry, my dear," Hughes said, being suave. "I had no idea that you were having such a bad day—"

"You're goddamned *right* you had no idea. You haven't called me and those triple-bleeping bleeps at Operations told me that I shouldn't call you."

"I *did* ask that no one call me," Hughes said. "I have a big problem and it's taking all of my time. I was *going* to call you when I had some free time."

"Oh shit, yes. You're always *going* to call me, but you never do. You're always *going* to see me, but it isn't for months. It's just the same old bullshit from you, over and over."

Hughes saw that he had her slightly calmed down, so he kept going. "Things will be different as soon as I can get rid of these business problems. Then we can spend a lot of time together. Just be patient and try to understand what I'm going through."

"Just be patient," she mimicked. "Just be patient and stay in this bleeping house all the time, don't go anywhere, don't *do* anything, don't talk to anyone except those quadruple-bleepers in Operations. This is really a shitty life you have me living."

"Let *me* call Operations," Hughes said, "and get them straightened out. Then I'll call you back."

"You can try," she said, "but I won't be here."

The chances of her really disappearing were slight, since there was a 24-hour-a-day guard at her house whose job it was to prevent her from escaping. Hughes called Operations.

"I've just been talking to the Party and she is very upset. The only request I ever make of you people is that you don't upset her, and yet she is always upset. Is it too much to ask of you that you follow my instructions and not let her get upset?"

"But Mr. Hughes," the staff man said. "We *try* not to upset her. *We* couldn't help it if the power went off. *We* couldn't help it if the cook couldn't get to work. Those were the things she was upset about today—"

"Why the hell *couldn't* the cook get to work?" Hughes wanted to know. "She is paid to be available on a 24-hour basis, and there is no reason that she shouldn't *be* there!"

"But Mr. Hughes, we've been having a terrible rainstorm and the canyons are blocked. There hasn't been a car up Coldwater in the last six hours."

Hughes turned around and looked at me. Yeah! I was wet. It *was* raining.

"Well," he said, "you find some way to get the cook up to the house so that the Party can have something to eat. Have her clean up the dogshit, too. Get going on this right now and try to have that cook up there within an hour." (This was a perfect example of Hughes's mind at work. Having been informed that the road was impassable, he then instructed someone to go up that road.)

Then he called the Party. "Honey, I just called Operations and told them to have the cook at your house within an hour. She'll fix dinner for you and clean up the dog's mess. Now just sit by the fireplace and relax and soon everything will be all right."

You had to hand it to the Party. She had some sense of reality, of what was possible in the middle of a giant storm, at around 1:00 in the morning, with the road outside her house looking like Niagara.

"Bullshit!" she shouted. "The bleeping cook won't be here until tomorrow! If you'd bother to look out the bleeping window you'd *see* that there's a bleeping flood! Don't *bother* to send anyone up here! *I'm leaving!*" Click.

Hughes called Operations. "Make certain that the guard at the Party's house is alert. She is threatening to run away again. I have you fellows to thank for that—if you did your job properly she wouldn't think of running away." (Another example of Hughes's straight thinking. How was Operations supposed to get in touch with the guard?)

After a while the phone rang in the bungalow. It was her. She sounded completely different. "I'm sorry for the way I acted," she said. "It's been a bad day and I let those unnaturally performing double-bleepers at Operations get to me. I didn't mean to upset you. I'm going to bed now and I'll feel better tomorrow." I couldn't believe the change of mood.

"I'm glad you're going to get some rest," said Hughes. "Don't forget to hold your breasts when you take off your bra. I'm sure that the cook will be there before you go to sleep, so let her stay there the night and she'll be

180

there when you need her tomorrow. Call me when she arrives so that I'll know everything is all right."

Oops! *"I don't want the cook up here!"* she screamed. "I'm going to bed and I won't let anyone in! *If anyone comes up here I won't let them in, I don't give a shit who it is!* Good-bye!"

Hughes sat quietly for a while and then picked up the phone. He dialed a number and I heard the phone ringing. No answer. He hung up and dialed again. This time he was calling Operations.

"I've just tried to call the Party and I don't get an answer," Hughes said. "Call the phone company and have them check to see that the phone is working. Call me back when you have this information."

That was all Pacific Telephone had to worry about. About three-quarters of an hour later the phone rang in the bungalow. The staff man reported, "It took a long time, Mr. Hughes, but the telephone people told us that the phone at that number was working perfectly."

"You call that number at five-minute intervals," Hughes said. "When the Party answers you tell her to call me at once."

About 15 minutes later Hughes called Operations again. "Goddamn it! I told you to call the Party and tell her to call me! Have you done it?"

"But Mr. Hughes, we've been calling as you instructed, and the phone rings, but there is no answer." Hughes hung up.

We sat for another half hour. No calls. Finally my old pal, my buddy, my employer, turned around and looked at me. "Ron, do you know the Party?"

I nodded yes. I had once been called away from a

dinner party so that I could deliver some flowers to her. It was raining that night, too.

"Ron, I hate to ask you to do this, but would you please take her a message for me?"

Shit! I was so quintuply bleeping tired that I couldn't move, my clothes were soaked, I was a candidate for the respiratory disease of the week, it was still pouring outside, you couldn't drive up the canyon, and even if you could, the Party wasn't going to answer the door, and weird Howard, all he wanted was for me to take a message up there. One thing, and one thing only, caused me to agree to go up there. *It would get me out of his room.*

I signaled him that I'd go. He sat there, thinking, and I realized that it wasn't going to be a simple delivery. He was cooking up a scheme.

"Ron, I don't want her to see your face. I want you to put your car-coat on and to pull the hood down to here." He held his fingers at the midpupil level of his eyes. "I want you to zip it all the way up and pull the front down to here." He held his fingers to a point just below his nose. "If you do that she won't be able to see your face." That was enough. More than enough. I cleared my throat.

"Why don't I just put the fucking thing on backwards?"

He looked sheepish. "I guess you're right, Ron, it really doesn't matter if she sees your face or not. Just go up there and tell her it is very important that she call me."

Since we weren't standing on formality that night, there was no need for me to wait until he called the Third Man to let me out. I walked to the door, opened it, waved to Hughes, and went to deliver the message.

The ride up the canyon was terrible. It wasn't that the

cops had blocked it off, but that anyone with sense was staying off the roads. The rivers of water were carrying down huge chunks of trees as well as a helluva lot of mud. It was almost daybreak when I pulled into her driveway. Her guard was parked near her house, sound asleep.

I went up to her front door and began to pound on it. No response. I waited for a half minute and started hammering again. Nothing. Then I began to kick the door as hard as I could. I think it would have been more effective if I hadn't had my wet Hush Puppies on. They tended to make a squishing noise when I kicked, but I kept pounding and kicking.

Finally the door opened a slight bit. The Party was standing there in a sheer nightgown. "What the fuck do you want?" she asked. She was always the lady.

"Call Hughes now," I said.

"Fuck you," she said. "I won't call the old sonofabitch."

I didn't much feel like arguing the point, but I had made an interesting observation. Her face was very flushed. Both sides of her neck were reddened just a bit. It looked like whisker burns. When I looked over her shoulder, I could see into one side of her bedroom. There was a pile of clothes there that seemed too big for one skinny girl.

"Listen," I rasped, "you either pick up the phone right now and call Mr. Hughes or I am going to go into your bedroom and take that guy by the hard-on and beat him to death with it!" I knew and she knew that she wasn't supposed to have *anyone* in that house, and especially not some stud.

"Okay," she said. "You can leave. I'll call him. I promise."

183

"Be sure you do," I said. I gave her my best smile, sloshed to my car, and let the downhill river carry me back to the hotel. I went to my room, took a long, hot shower, came out, drank a half-pint of bourbon, and ordered some food through Operations. As I sat and waited for the food to be delivered, the phone rang. It was Hughes.

"Ron, I don't know what you told the Party, but I sure do appreciate it. She called me, we had a nice long talk, and everything is just great. I want to thank you very much." I started to say something in reply, do my bashful-boy routine, but it was too late. He hung up. My reward was a three-day respite from the bungalow.

Hughes was to get no long relief from the Party. Their phone calls were becoming monologues in which she would complain about his turning her into a recluse, about her wanting to get out and live it up, and about her career: After all, she *had* been promised stardom. It became clear that Hughes would either have to find something for her to do to occupy her time or else she would try one escape attempt too many and get away. Hughes instructed his right-hand man Bill Gay to think of something for the Party to do. Finally, in a conference, they decided that the Party should become a singing star. (I don't know if Hughes had ever screened *Citizen Kane* and remembered the sequence in which the powerful publisher tried to turn his young inamorata into an opera star.)

A top-drawer writing team was hired to create an original song, one that would complement the voice and delivery of the Party. A tune was finally delivered that satisfied all concerned. It had taken some time to get the song, and it took just as long to get the orchestra. It wasn't possible to obtain the services of a big-name band, since this project was taking so long that any successful band would have had to cancel most of its bookings on the road.

Ultimately, it was decided to hire a society orchestra from L.A.—one of those groups that specializes in debutante balls and the like. This was to be the *best* band specializing in la-de-da affairs. It was necessary, though, for the orchestra to hold a lot of practice sessions, which in turn had to be scheduled around other appearances. The Party was informed of all of this but was more than content to wait while everything fell into place. After all, a lot of time, money, and energy were being pumped into her first record. Not the least of it was the choice of recording studio, a place on Santa Monica Boulevard in Hollywood that was known to be the best studio in the business.

Naturally, using that studio meant more delays, since it was booked solidly by some of the biggest names in the music world. Weeks and weeks passed, and the orchestra, singer, and studio hadn't all been brought together.

Finally it happened. The orchestra was available, the studio was available, and God knows the singer was available. (It should be mentioned that rehearsals are usually held in *rehearsal halls,* rather than in more expensive, less available recording studios.) The practice sessions were scheduled for the late afternoons, since the Party habitually went to bed late and got up around noon. (Operations was instructed to have a parking spot available for the Party within a few feet of the studio, a difficult task during the late-afternoon rush hour. A couple of times no space was there, the Party complained, and some severe ass-chewing by Hughes resulted.)

The rehearsals dragged on and on. Minor changes were made in the music, lyrics, and orchestral arrangement. A voice coach was brought in solely to help the Party with the lyrics. All of these changes were reported to Hughes by the Party. All of this had served its purpose —she had calmed down and was no longer threatening to run away. It allowed Hughes to concentrate on his business affairs. The bad news was that it had become routine for the Party to sing a few bars of the song to Hughes when she spoke to him. She was god-awful! But Hughes would listen and would often ask that she repeat a line or two. He pretended to love each moment of it; either he was a great actor or tone deaf or, come to think of it, had turned down the volume of his hearing aid.

Finally it was time to cut the record. I have no idea how many takes it took before the product was considered finished, but it was reported to Hughes that it was ready for the world. Ah, but was the world ready? If everyone else was like me in terms of musical taste, the answer was no.

One of the worst nights I ever spent in that bungalow was the night the Party got her first pressing of the record. She could hardly wait to get Hughes on the phone and play the record for him—over and over and over. The melody was okay, the lyrics were okay, the arrangement was okay, but the singer was dreadful. She was so bad that I thought her voice alone, played over a loudspeaker, would have kept the swallows from coming back to Capistrano. When I went back to my room I was disgusted by what I had heard, but I figured that that was about the last I'd hear of the song. Was I foolish!

The next morning I flipped on a radio as I was getting up. Imagine my shock when the deejay introduced a *fine* new singer, a *wonderful* new record, and then played the Party's recording. It wasn't to end there. The record was played on that station with depressing regularity for the next week. From the exposure you would have guessed that the record had sold a million copies. Hardly.

But its exposure wasn't ended in L.A. The Party was to be rewarded for her recent good conduct and hard work by being allowed to take her parents and younger brother to visit relatives in New Mexico. That little vacation was a thrill for her to plan. It was a nightmare for the Hughes organization. After all, she had become accustomed to hearing her record played several times a day over one of the major L.A. radio stations. She would certainly expect a hit in L.A. to be a hit in Albuquerque, and in all the other towns she drove through on her way to New Mexico.

The record's being on the radio was one thing. But it also had to be placed in the stores. A huge quantity of records was shipped to Albuquerque. These were distributed to every store that handled 45s within a hundred miles of the Party's relatives. When she got back from the trip she was really excited about the exposure her record was getting. I guess she assumed that if it was a hit in Barstow, Gallup, Flagstaff, and Albuquerque, it must have been a hit in New York, Boston, Chicago, and Atlanta. (I don't know if she noticed a lack of royalty checks . . . or if she got those, too!)

There was one more bit of unpleasantness for Hughes. He got a call from the Major. It seemed that her sister had read an article in one of the music trade papers that said Howard Hughes had invested over $250,000 in the creation of a new singing star. Her first record was out and not selling. Furthermore, the piece said that certain disc jockeys in L.A.—and I needn't say which station— had each become the proud possessors of two round-trip airline tickets to Rome. They were to fly, first-class, via TWA and enjoy first-class accommodations throughout their stay in Italy. It took a lot of talking for Hughes to finesse his way out of that one.

Finally, though, the Party caused him one great bit of trouble. Putting it bluntly, she wanted a lot more out of men, sexually, than an occasional visit in a hotel bungalow. Somehow she managed to elude her guard and disappeared. Operations called Hughes to tell him, which resulted in some interesting criticism by Hughes. (The Party might have benefited in her choice of obscenities by hearing that conversation.) But then Hughes got the red-alert call. Walter Kane, his talent scout, had been visited by the Party and a male companion. The man had been armed and had strongly suggested that he and the Party have a little meeting with Hughes. Then other calls began to be reported by Operations. Other members of the Hughes organization had been visited by the same guy and the Party, each time to suggest that there be a meeting with Hughes. It didn't take an idiot to figure out that since she knew he was in a bungalow, something was going to happen there.

The first thing that happened was Bungalow Four's being put under full-time guard. These weren't drivers or the Third Man, but Operations staff people. I became involved when I walked back to my room from the bungalow and found Bishop Lundeen sitting there. He figured that if he was going to have to walk around the bungalow, he was going to share my room. I hate uninvited guests, so I did something immediately that I figured would get rid of him. I produced a jug of bourbon. Then I went to the drugstore and bought the cheapest cigars in the house. Then I went back upstairs and drank and smoked those cheapo cigars.

He was sitting there reading a book about accounting. I recognized the book from college—it was a basic accounting text. That really got me. Lundeen was in charge of the leasing of houses for Hughes and was involved in the spending of heaven only knows how much money, and there he was studying basic accounting. It took about a day for my drinking and smoking to drive him out of the room.

A couple of days later the situation came to a head. It was about 2:00 in the morning, and I had gotten a call to report to the bungalow. I noticed as I walked over there that the guard detail seemed to have disappeared, which I thought odd. As I stood on the patio, waiting for the Third Man to let me in, I had a queasy feeling, and then I felt something coming at me in the darkness. As I turned I saw a shape coming off the lawn and at me. I swung around, and as I raised my arm I hit the person across the chest. It was the Party, and her momentum plus the force of my blow knocked her clear off the patio and back onto the lawn. She started swearing at me and I looked behind her; there was a torpedo with a .38 in his belt.

I stuck my hand into my coat pocket, as though I had a gun, and stared at him. Those next five seconds seemed like five years. If he called my bluff I was a dead man and so was Hughes—after all, *the bungalow door still was never locked.* Then the guy picked the Party up off the lawn, and the two of them went back toward Crescent Drive, got in a car, and drove away. A few minutes later the Third Man showed up and let me into the bungalow. I didn't say anything about what had happened, either to the Third Man, or to Hughes.

A day or so later, though, Hughes mentioned the incident. Evidently someone from Operations who was staying at the hotel saw what was happening and then reported it to Hughes. (That of itself is pretty bizarre, because he was reporting, in effect, that Operations hadn't been doing its job.) In any case, Hughes said to me, "I understand that you were in the right place at the right time the other night, and you handled yourself very well, and I just want you to know that I appreciate it."

Chapter 15

You might think that having proven to Hughes my ability to be there when he needed me, I would be called on in every crisis. But that wasn't quite the case. There was, for example, the matter of the Easter Sunday fly.

Hughes pretended not to notice any legal holidays. This was in keeping with his extremely irregular hours but was extremely transparent to all of us who were close to him. If a holiday was just another day, then why did the Old Man go so far out of his way to make sure all of us were on duty for those days? The obvious answer is that we were the family he never had. We showed him the affection and comradeship that he never knew, growing up orphaned and rich and a long-time bachelor.

Holidays were hell for us. All of us had family gatherings which we either had to miss or visit for a short time. In either case, a lot of strain was put on relationships that meant a great deal to us. That was probably why Johnnie Holmes had begun lobbying for a free day on Easter as early as Christmas. Hughes finally relented and assured Johnnie that that day would be his to spend with his family.

On Easter Sunday I was on duty, and I wasn't surprised to see Hughes pick up the phone and call Holmes. The Old Man launched into a transparent con: "Johnnie, I know I promised you that you could have this Easter Sunday with your family, but I have to interrupt your day. This won't take long, but I have to have you come down here. There's a fly in my room." I don't know who was more pissed off with that excuse, Holmes—a Catholic—or me. After all, I was a pretty good flycatcher.

Johnnie came into the bungalow a couple of flyless hours later. (I had been sitting there alertly, but I saw *no fly* in that room.) He was a good actor, so he wasn't showing the displeasure he must have been feeling. He stood in front of Hughes, who said in his most apologetic tone of voice, "I'm sorry, John, but there's a fly somewhere in here and I just *have* to turn to *you* to catch it." The humidity in the room went up about 15 percent because I was sitting there, steaming: You can get me to do a lot of bullshit things, but don't *ever* tell me I'm not doing them well.

Holmes began his search, looking everywhere he could walk. He worked slowly, very slowly. After 45 minutes of brilliant acting, he made his way alongside Hughes's chair, out of the Old Man's range of vision but well within mine. Johnnie looked at me, tapped his forehead and smiled, then reached into his breast pocket and pulled out a Kleenex. He opened it up and tilted it gingerly towards me. Resting on the tissue was the corpse of a big, beautiful fly. *The cheating sonofabitch had brought one from home!*

He put the fly away and worked his way to a far corner of the room, where Hughes could watch him only by twisting around and looking over his shoulder. Then Holmes made a big production out of spotting a fly. He put a piece of fresh Kleenex on his hand. Ready for the kill! He made a pass at the supposed fly and then sub-stituted the Kleenex he had brought from home for the one in his hand. It was neatly done. Then he went over to Hughes.

"Did you get him, John?" asked Hughes. Holmes nod-ded. "Well, let's have a look." Holmes unfolded the Kleenex very carefully, and then placed his hand so that the dead body was right in front of Hughes's face. The Old Man really studied that dead fly.

Finally Hughes said, "Johnnie, that's a nice fly." Holmes nodded, smiling. Then Hughes looked up thoughtfully and said, "Next time, John, let's get a *legal* kill." He *knew* that Holmes had cheated and yet we were all close enough to understand the joke, so we all broke out in hysterical laughter for the next five minutes. When the laughter had subsided, Hughes said, "John, go on and spend the rest of the day with your family and a Happy Easter to you."

Holmes may have distinguished himself in The Case of the Previously Killed Fly, but I had *my* moment in The Matter of the Fouled-up Steno Notebooks. It came dur-ing a day so balmy and beautiful that I was inwardly cursing myself for not having devised a way to get to the beach. In the middle of the morning, Operations called Hughes to inform him that it had a grave problem. (Hughes had created Operations to take care of *his* prob-lems, but evidently they thought it was a two-way street.)

The root of the difficulty was what had happened when Noah Dietrich had left the Hughes organization. That night every lock at the Romaine Street building was changed. One of the people who had a key, and an office inside, was a movie honcho—it was never clear to me whether he was a director or producer—who was work-ing on a project for Hughes Productions. Well, when this guy arrived at the building the morning after Dietrich left, he found he couldn't get in. In fact, he learned that not only was he locked out, but that his project was at an end and that he would not *ever* be allowed back inside. His work *and* his personal effects were inside, and he was outside. No amount of pleading with staff changed the situation, and the guy went into a slow burn that culminated in a law suit against the Hughes organization. The action had kicked around the courts and had finally been settled, out of court, while we were at Nosseck's. The guy was to be paid some money for his inconvenience, *and* he'd finally be allowed to recover his personal effects. *That* was where the problem lay.

Among the other items in the guy's desk were 12 steno notebooks that had been used by his secretary for dictation. She had saved them in case she needed them for reference. After the guy was locked out, someone in the Hughes organization had found the notebooks and decided it would be a good idea to microfilm their contents. In order to facilitate the filming, the wires holding the books together had been cut. Then the single sheets of paper had been filmed, replaced in order, and bound back together by rubber bands. But rubber bands do not resemble spiral wires, a fact of no account *until* the guy won the right to get those books back from Hughes Productions. Then it became a priority project to get those books back to their original condition, so that the guy would never know that they had been filmed.

The grave problem, as explained by a staff man, went like this: "So-and-so is going to pick up his property tomorrow, Mr. Hughes, but his secretarial notepads have been taken apart. We've called every wire manufacturer in the city, but none of them has the spiral wire necessary to put the books back together. We've called an eastern manufacturer and he is going to send us some wire, but we're afraid that it won't get here in time. We don't know what to do."

As I listened to this bedraggled tale of woe I watched the back of Hughes's neck, looking for signs of an impending explosion (*he* was sweating out the TWA deal and *they* were bothering him with notebook wire). But he seemed to accept it in stride. Very calmly he asked for the staff man to repeat the problem. Then Hughes repeated what he had been told back to the man at Operations. Then Hughes said something that took me aback.

"My," he said, and he really sounded sincere, "you really *do* have a big problem there. I'm so glad you called me about it, and I *do* want to help you find a solution. I want to help so much, in fact, that I'm going to send Ron to help you with your big problem. You make certain to assist him in every way that you can."

With that he hung up and turned to face me. "Ron, I'm sure that you have heard these conversations. Now that you know what their problem is, would you go and take care of it?" I gave him my yes nod and went to the door to wait for the Third Man to be summoned.

I drove over to Operations, honked, and waited for a face to appear in the window upstairs. One of the staff started to let the fishline down so that I could write him a note, but I decided to be an asshole. I shouted up, "Just bring me those goddamned books!" (It always pissed off the staff when you hollered instead of playing with their little fishline.) A couple of minutes later one of the staff bozos came out with a cardboard box. In it was the problem, the 12 steno notebooks. As he handed me the box he asked me what I was going to do. I smiled at him, got in my car, and left. I drove up to Hollywood Boulevard and parked near the local F. W. Woolworth.

Inside I found the stationery department and bought 12 steno notepads. Cost: $3.12. Then I went to the hardware department and picked up a pair of needle-nose pliers. Cost: $2.08. Then I went to the drivers' room. I took the pliers and straightened out one end of the spiral wire that held a new book together and then I twisted the wire out of the holes, so that it was free from all the pages. Next I took one of the old pads, removed the rubber band, and inserted the new wire, twisting it until the old book was held by the new wire. Then I closed the end of the wire I had twisted open. It took me about a half an hour to do all 12 books. They looked as if nothing had ever happened to them.

Then I drove around to the front of Operations, honked, and waited. When the face appeared I shouted up, "Here're your fucking books," got out of the car, deposited the box on the sidewalk, and drove away. I looked in my rear-view mirror to see a staff man scurrying out to pick up the priceless box. Then I headed out toward Malibu, where I had a fine lobster lunch. After a few hours I drove back to the hotel.

Hughes called me back to the bungalow a short time later. As I walked in he asked me, "Ron, did you take care of that big problem?" I nodded yes. He asked, "What did you do—buy some new steno pads and use the wires from them?" Once more I nodded yes. Hughes smiled, "I thought you would. Thanks."

There was only one more thing to do before the incident was closed. Hughes called Operations.

"Did you get the steno pads back?"

"Yes, Mr. Hughes."

"Are they in condition to return to the owner?"

"Yes, Mr. Hughes."

"Well, isn't that *nice*. I'm so *glad* you called me with

your problem. If you have any *other* pressing problems, be *sure* to call and tell me about them . . . AND I'LL HAVE RON TAKE CARE OF THEM FOR YOU!" Then he slammed down the receiver so hard I thought he had broken the thing. He let me out of the bungalow early that day, and I went to the Polo Lounge for cocktails. Funny, but I didn't get a call from Operations all the time I was in the bar.

The loathing between Operations and me was surely mutual. I regarded them as a bunch of witless creeps, and I figure they saw me as a Gentile rowdy who was a constant threat to their rules and regulations. The situation was inflamed because my duties were shared with another person, a staff man named Howard Eckersley. Eckersley was supposed to be available so that I would be able to take breathers. In practice, I worked about 70 percent of the time and Eckersley was in Bungalow Four about 30 percent of the time. But I didn't dislike him just because I was spending more time with Hughes.

Because Eckersley was brass and I was just an enlisted man, he could break the rules that I had to live under. When *I* was off-duty I was supposed to stay in my room. Under no circumstances was I supposed to spend time at the pool or playing tennis. You can guess where I would see Eckersley as I went to and from the bungalow during the daytime—the pool and the tennis courts. While he was poolside he would entertain a constant stream of visitors, whereas I was supposed to allow no guests to visit me except my wife, and her only in the privacy of my room.

Having two sets of rules was bad enough, but Eckersley was constantly trying to impress the Old Man with *his* dedication and with the fact that Ron was breaking rules and generally not doing his job well. I expect he could have got more mileage out of that stuff except that he kept tripping himself up by reporting things he heard and saw in the bungalow to Operations—things that Operations could only have learned from Eckersley. Again, it was understandable that Operations wanted information. What was peculiar was the way they were forced to get it.

Actually, there were a lot of things they were better off not knowing. The staff attitude towards Hughes was one of such veneration and awe that they had no perspective whatever about the nature of their jobs and their relationship with their employer. Their blind obedience and hero worship seemed unhealthy to me. Whenever they had to confront reality with Hughes, it was a shock.

There was an occasion when Hughes had to sign a memorandum. (It was the only time I ever saw him even entertain the notion of signing anything.) The memo was the capper to the TWA loan, an acknowledgment that he would abide by certain rules laid down by the parties putting up the money. Anyway, a staff man named Paul Wynn was selected to come to the bungalow to get this thing signed. When Wynn entered the bungalow it was obvious to me that he had gone out and bought himself a brand-new suit for the occasion. I was especially taken with the fact that he was wearing a nice little hat. Of course, in southern California if you see a guy with a hat on, you hail his cab or get on his bus—no one wears hats around L.A.

Hughes told him to freeze when Wynn got in front of him. I don't know what Wynn expected, but there he was standing in front of a crusty old gent whose hair was down his back and whose beard was down his front and whose only apparel consisted of that pink napkin. I could tell that Wynn was as much transfixed by the room (the stacks of newspapers and magazines had grown as we stayed there until they were six and seven feet high, so that Hughes was forced to spend hours counterbalancing them) as his employer. As Wynn took it all in, he began to get very pale. I thought he very well might pass out or throw up. His idol was smashed. And of course *I* sat back there thumbing my nose at the guy. I'm sure that Wynn reported that as an act of disrespect toward the Old Man; Wynn certainly remembered the occasion later, when we had our last go-round.

The hostility between Operations and me came to a head, in terms of Eckersley, in the matter of Hughes's naps. The rules for working in the bungalow were simple: Sit quietly, and when the Old Man wanted a film shown, run the projector. The fact that he might call for reel one on Tuesday and reel two on Friday was of no matter. We were expected to be sitting there as ready on Friday as we were three days earlier. The only break was when Hughes ate or slept. Then we'd be allowed out, presumably to follow his lead: When he ate, we were supposed to eat, and when he slept, we were supposed to get *our* sleep. The naps screwed everything up. The extended phone calls Hughes was having about TWA so tired him that he began to take naps in his chair.

These snoozes lasted from a half an hour to four hours. While he was comfortable in that leather chair, picking up his Zs, I was sitting on an armless patio chair. So I decided to make a fight of it. One day Hughes announced to me that he was about to take a nap and that I should, too. I went for my notebook and wrote out a message: "I would like to go to my room when you take a nap." I got up, went over to Hughes, and stuck the pad under his nose so he could read it.

After a time for reading and a time for considering, he

looked at me and said, "Ron, I'm just going to take a short nap. Now I want you to go back to your chair and sit there. I will turn out the light and we both can take a short nap." The battle was on. It was obvious to me that Eckersley would gladly sit there until hell froze over if Hughes said to, so that any chance of getting out of that room while Hughes slept rested with me.

I wrote another note. "Your chair is one hell of a lot more comfortable than mine. I would like to go to my room so that I may smoke, go to the bathroom, and call my wife. I can be back here within five minutes after you call me." Hughes looked at the note and then gave me his best pissed-off look.

"We'll talk about it another time. We are going to take a short nap, you in your chair and me in mine. There are no real reasons for you to go to your room, but there are many reasons that I want you to go to your chair and sit down."

I was astonished to hear my own voice. "I am not going to go to that chair to take a nap. I am going to my room and will come back here as quickly as your nap is over and you call me."

Hughes chose to ignore the fact that I had spoken. But his voice was charged with emotion. "There is not a good reason in the world that would prevent you from going to your chair and doing what I'm asking you to do. *Now do it!*"

I wasn't about to stop. "Bullshit! I am not going to sit in a goddamned straight-backed chair with no arms and try to take a nap. I can't sleep that way. Besides, right now I have to take a shit." That was a pretty sleazy trick for me to pull, since I knew that the king of the enema couldn't deny me the right to move my bowels.

I was kept out of the bungalow for a couple of days. That is, he didn't call for me, which I knew was punishment and a chance for him to marshal his arguments. The next time I was called for I knew I was going to be nailed. The instant I walked in the room Hughes spoke up.

"Ron, just stand right where you are. Now, the last time you were in this room you talked! I have asked you not to talk and I want to remind you that it is important that you follow my instructions. I was also very displeased with your attitude concerning my naps. The next time that I ask you to take a short nap when I do, I will expect you to make an old man happy and comply. Howard does it and I fail to see any reason for you not to do likewise."

I was prepared for Hughes. I reached into my pocket and pulled out a note that thankfully anticipated Hughes's little lecture. It read, "I will not apologize for my actions. I will not stay in this room while you nap. I have not had to do it in the past and will not do it in the future. Sorry." He read the note and didn't say anything. Since he didn't take a nap that day, the issue didn't come up.

The next time I saw staff man Eckersley I jumped on him for turning a bad situation into an intolerable one. He barely deigned to acknowledge the fact that I was talking, and I found myself shouting, "For Christ's sake, the next thing he'll want you to do will be to bring your jammies in and sleep there." Eckersley looked at me and said, "Well, what's wrong with that?" I knew then that there was *no* common meeting ground.

It was quite some time later that Hughes again tried to nap with me in the room. He announced himself and quickly turned out the light. I stood up and went over to the door, trying to figure a way that I could walk out of there without disturbing the Old Man. A few minutes later, Hughes turned on the light.

In a soft, gentle voice he said, "Ron, please sit down. I want to talk to you." I took my seat. "I know that you're uncomfortable, that the hours are long and irregular, that you haven't been home with your family for a long time, and that I make you nervous, but I just want you to know how much I appreciate having you here. You do such good work, and always with a good-natured attitude, that it really helps my spirits to have you in the room with me. There isn't anyone in the whole world that I would rather have in this room with me than you, Ron."

It was his Sunday punch. He knew it was bullshit, I knew it was bullshit, but there we were, him laying it out and me taking it in. He was *so* maudlin in tone with this one that I began to smile. Evidently he saw that the speech had gone beyond belief, for he started grinning back at me.

"Ron, I wouldn't insult you with money. I can only promise you that you will have a job with me for the rest of your life. I know that I've been too tough on you and I apologize. You can go to your room. I'll send for you when I need you." It was my final victory in the matter of naps.

It was just about my final victory, period. Over a period of weeks I had begun to realize that I had a real physical problem. I had been having an itching sensation in my rectal area that was getting worse and worse. I had tried all the patent medicines with no relief, and I knew —when I was unable to make love with my wife on her visits or to sleep a full night's sleep—that I would have to see a doctor. In desperation I wrote a note to Hughes, saying, "I'm afraid I must see a doctor. I have a problem with my rectum." Hughes, however, felt that you go to a doctor to catch something, not cure it. He wanted to know what it was I had. Hemorrhoids? No. Piles? No. A rash? No. Finally he allowed as how he'd make arrangements for me to see a specialist.

Two weeks later I was still waiting. The itching was awful and the calls from Virgie, wanting to know why I hadn't yet seen a doctor, were almost as bad. I tried another note. "My ass is killing me and I want to see a doctor." Hughes glowered at me, and I glowered right back. Finally he said, "I've been making arrangements and should have word for you by tomorrow." When tomorrow came he was sleeping, all day. The day after that I was called back into the bungalow. I had brought a note with me, and I stuck it under his nose when I walked in. "When the hell do I get to see a doctor?" I was furious and he knew it. He called Operations and had them make an emergency appointment with one of the leading plumbing experts in Beverly Hills. I felt better almost instantly.

I was scheduled for the next day, and when I got to the doctor's office I was most impressed and even a little hesitant about putting my diseased bottom on one of his designer chairs. After checking me out, he asked about my job, diet, sleep habits, and the like. When he heard how I worked and what strain I was under, he diagnosed my problem as a "million-dollar rectum." It seems that the anal area is a nerve center, and when the body is plagued with severe nervous anxiety it is not uncommon for there to be a minor breakdown in a nerve center. The doctor told me that this condition was fairly typical among some of his more wealthy patients. (Hah!) The prescription was simple—and welcome: I was to go home and stay there for three to four weeks.

The next day when Hughes read my note—I had assured him in it that the doctor thought that what I was suffering was only mental and that I'd be as good as new in a month—he reacted with a simple statement.

"We'll get a new doctor," he said.

The next day I was sent to another specialist. He diagnosed my problem as a minor skin rash. I was sent to a dermatologist for treatments that consisted of ultraviolet light and calcium injections. But it didn't help. There was no such thing as sleep, and Hughes began to really put it to me: long, long sessions with little free time. He was getting meaner than hell. To top everything off, Virgie had called and told me that while she liked having checks for $464 delivered to her every week by one of the drivers, she'd rather have a full-time husband. It was a choice between Hughes and her. Having delivered her ultimatum, she took the family up to the beach at Carpenteria, near Santa Barbara, to enjoy the September warmth. (It generally gets hot in southern California in the fall.)

I took off from the hotel and got incredibly drunk. But being loyal, I did check in from time to time so that the Old Man wouldn't have a fit like the other time I got juiced. One of the check-ins took place in a very stuffy phone booth in the San Fernando Valley. That was a toll call from the main Operations number, so I had to go through the operator. When I asked her to connect me, she said, "Oh! Are you a Hughes man?"

I was stunned. "No," I said. "I was just given this number to call. What is it?"

"It's Operations for Howard Hughes," she said.

"How do you know that?" I wondered.

"Well," she said, "I handle a lot of calls for Mr. Eckersley and Mr. Bench and Mr. Carlisle."

The phone was ringing all this time, and in my drunken mind I kept thinking that she was filling me in on details she had no right to know. Then some toad in Operations answered the ring. His first line was, "Ron, have you been drinking?"

"Look asshole, I called, didn't I? Am I due back at the hotel or what?"

"Ron, for heck sakes, we've asked you not to drink. You do work for Mr. Hughes and you *are* in a position of being extremely hot, and we don't want you to talk to anyone about anything."

I was hot, all right. It was about 110 degrees in that booth, and all I could think of was that I was being lectured to while the guys in Operations were letting phone-company operators know what they were doing. So I told the guy where to get off and hung up.

The next day I woke up with a hangover and a half. I was in the bed at my house, and the phone woke me up. It was Paul Wynn calling from Operations. He wanted me to know I had to get back to the hotel.

"Paul," I said, "I want some food in my room when I get there." And I gave him the order, because I know that for me, food helps a hangover. Then I raced back to the hotel and went to my room. No food. I called room service and they told me they hadn't gotten an order from Wynn.

So I called him at Operations, and he got real cutesy with me. He was getting his revenge for my nose-thumbing. "Oh, for heaven's sake! Didn't they get your food to you? Poor Ronnie doesn't have anything to eat?" If he had been where I could have gotten my hands on him I would have broken him into little globules of fat, and he knew it.

Then my phone rang. I was wanted in the bungalow.

I tried to hold out for food, but it was important that I get over there. When I walked in it must have been 90 degrees in that room. Hughes smelled like a goat, or perhaps it was just the accumulation in the room that smelled bad. I sat in my chair, and he announced it was time for a nap. I couldn't keep from jumping up and giving him a note saying that it was just too damned hot in there. I don't know why I didn't complain about the nap *first*. My brain wasn't in the best of shape.

He read it, and then finally he told me that I could turn the air conditioner on to its very lowest position. Well, the very lowest setting on air conditioners in those days was one click above "noise." Another ten minutes went by. I wrote another note saying that it was *still* too hot in there for anyone with clothes on. He picked up a book of matches and said that I could turn the cold control up about half the thickness of the matchbook. That really began to piss me off. Fun is fun, but I was sitting there with an acute hangover, I was hungry, and it was intolerably hot.

Then he turned off his hearing aid *and* the light. "Ron, just sit there quietly while I take a short nap." That did it. I went and stood by the door, and he finally turned on the light and told me to go back and sit down. I just stood there. He went to the other side of the room and began playing with some stacks of papers. I thought that the time had come when I wasn't going to take any more shit. I picked up a large Turkish towel and began fanning at him.

What with his bare ass hanging out, he felt what I was doing and he might have thought that I was physically going to come after him. He went back to his chair, and I lost control. I started screaming at him.

"Goddamned crazy old bastard! It's so goddamned

hot in here you could fry an egg on the floor and *still* you won't turn on the air conditioner! I'm sick and you make the doctor tell me a bunch of lies! You told me that I wouldn't have to stay in this damned room when you took a nap!

"My wife is leaving me and taking the kids! You've got *me* half-crazy now! You run around nude in this stinking shithole and I'm leaving before I get as nuts as you are!

"FUCK YOU, HOWARD HUGHES! I QUIT!"

Hughes's eyebrows were arched, his eyes bulging. He could hear me, all right. I knew that my face was red and my veins were popping; that's how I am when I get angry.

I walked over to the door and grabbed the private, privileged doorknob with my bare hand. I flung the door open as wide as it would go. The Third Man was in Bungalow One. There was no one around to brush at the flies. I looked back to see Hughes sitting, nude, in that damned old white leather chair. He was shielding his eyes from the sunlight, something that he hadn't seen in months. He was also reaching for the telephone, probably to call the Third Man.

It was around noon on Sunday, and there were streams of people walking along the sidewalk outside the bungalow, going to or coming from the Polo Lounge or the pool. Most of them in the vicinity as I came out heard the sharp sound of the door slamming open and they peered into the gloom of Bungalow Four, trying to see who that poor skinny old mole was, the one with the beard and the hair and the pink napkin stuffed in his crotch.

I haven't seen Howard Hughes since.

207

Epilogue

I went to my room, threw my clothes, toilet articles, and booze into a suitcase, swept my paperback library into a pillowcase, and then, having finished packing, called Operations and asked for Kay Glenn. It was Sunday, so they had to chase him down, but he called back in a few minutes.

"Kay," I said, "I want you to get this straight from me. When Hughes calls, he's going to tell you about my recent actions, and what he'll say will be absolutely correct. I told him to go fuck himself and that I quit."

There was a silence so long that I began to think the line had gone dead. Finally Kay said, "Ron, you can't *quit.*" Just like that. Indentured servitude wasn't dead. It was alive and flourishing at Hughes Productions. There was nothing that Glenn could have said that would have angered me more, so I told him what he could do with the problem. After all, I had told the Old Man that I was quitting and I didn't think that I needed to justify it to some employee of Hughes.

Finally I decided to give Glenn what at the time seemed to me to be the coup de grace, so I told him, "I'm leaving this hotel *now,* and I'm going to join my family on the *beach*. When we leave there we're going to drive through *Nevada* on our way to Colorado, and there's not a goddamned thing you can do about it." (The beach, for some unknown reason, was out of bounds to Hughes employees. Nevada, of course, was off limits because of the nuclear testing that was underway at the time.) Then I hung up and left the hotel. Since I had never formally registered, it didn't seem to me to be necessary to let the front desk know I was leaving.

When I stopped by my house to pick up some clothes that would fit in at Carpenteria, the phone was ringing. It was Operations, saying that it was very important that I talk with Mr. Bill Gay *right then* and that I should call Gay. I told the guy that he might find inner happiness by using the phone as a suppository and hung up. Two minutes later Gay called me.

"Ron, Kay Glenn has told me of your disgraceful actions in front of Mr. Hughes. I'm very disappointed in your actions, but I will deal with you in that matter at a later time. I want you to go back to the hotel and go to your room and wait for further orders." It seemed to me that Gay was, typically, ignoring my side of what had happened. In fact, he was ignoring the central point.

"Bill," I said, wanting him to wince at someone calling him by his first name, "I told Howard Hughes, I repeated it to Kay Glenn, and I will tell you, one time only, *I quit.*"

"You *can't* quit. Now you get back to the hotel as I told you to do. You'd better hurry before you get into *more* trouble with Mr. Hughes."

How could I deal with that kind of thinking? He had pissed me off by calling, and his line of reasoning hadn't helped matters. I had waited a long time to tell him what I thought of him.

"Bill, *fuck you!* Fuck Kay Glenn. Fuck Howard Hughes.

Fuck Hughes Productions. Fuck everything. *I quit.*"
Then I hung up.

When I got to Carpenteria I found my family camped
in a state campground. After dinner, when the kids were
asleep, I told Virgie about what had happened. Her spirits picked up with the telling, and she agreed that I surely
had the *right* to quit. I had never signed a contract with
Hughes Productions, I had never made an oral promise
to work for Hughes for the rest of my life, and the only
operative thing seemed to be the Old Man's promise that
I would have a job as long as I lived. I assumed that my
quitting took care of *that*.

We spent about five more days at the beach, and then
went back to our house to get ready for the trip to
Colorado. We hadn't been there very long when the
phone rang. It was Kay Glenn, calling at the personal
direction of Bill Gay. Glenn was to transmit to me a
personal message from Hughes. It went as follows: "I am
not upset with you. I know that I have worked you too
long, too hard, and under the most difficult conditions.
I know that you are not in the best of health. I would like
to apologize for these problems. I want you to stay home
and rest up until you hear from me."

There was no doubt in my mind that the message came
from Hughes. Glenn was so nice on the phone that I felt
he had had additional orders from Hughes on how to
treat me. It felt nice to win a round, but I was still ready
to head to Colorado and catch up on autumn.

"Kay, I'm leaving for Colorado within the next couple
of days. I'll be gone for two or three weeks and I'd like
to have my paycheck mailed to an address that I'll mail
you. I'll let you know when I get back." I thought the
check I was talking about was most probably the last one

I'd ever get, but *I* wasn't about to mention the magic words "final check."

Glenn wasn't about to give up completely. "Ron, Mr. Hughes asked that you stay at *home* and wait to hear from him."

"Kay, I'll *mail* you the address for my check. You'll hear from me later." Kay was trying to tell me to at least stay out of Nevada when I hung up.

After a wonderful three-week vacation (marred only by the continued itching), I got home to discover that I was still on the payroll. I was being paid $125 a week, which wasn't enough to pay the bills. (I was still seeing a doctor in Beverly Hills for the itch, but those bills were being picked up by the Hughes organization.) My contacts with Operations were at a minimum. I had nothing to say to them, and they had no messages from Hughes. I got very bored and fairly broke, so I took a job in a high-class Chinese restaurant (owned by film star Phillip—"Yank, you die"—Ahn) as a 2:00 A.M.–6:00 A.M. janitor. It paid $200 a month, which was enough to keep me in beer. I figured I could get by with the job, since it was late at night.

After a few months I began to do a hell of a lot in the way of soul-searching. On the one hand, it seemed that Hughes would have to call. On the other, I had heard of people who had been at home for as long as *20 years,* waiting for that call. They were being paid—probably more than me—and they seemed to enjoy their lives. While my family liked having me around, I wondered just how much they'd like it if I were *always* there. The alternative was to go out and look for work, hampered by my itch.

I decided to lay back for a while longer, under the

assumption that something would turn up in the organization. (I figured I was still under the wing of the Old Man, even if the clucks in Operations didn't care for me.) I knew there were good jobs, cushy ones, to be had. I certainly didn't want to go back to what I had been doing, since it appeared that the Old Man had no intentions of ever going back into the outside world.

Then I got a call from a guy I had worked with at Kraft Foods. He wondered if I'd be interested in selling chain-link fences. It was a new field for me, and his boss agreed to take me on for a month on a no-salary trial basis. It was a better job than chasing stray grains of rice, and I began to earn a good living, especially since I was still being paid by Hughes.

The best news of all came when I visited another, non-Beverly Hills, nonspecialist, doctor. After a short interview the doctor told me what I seemed to have: pinworms. Common, ordinary pinworms. I was put on medication that cured the problem in a fairly short time. (I did call the distinguished doctor in Beverly Hills to tell him that the man he had unsuccessfully treated, twice a week, for months, was being cured. Beverly Hills is not the pinworm center of the universe, so he was almost as mystified when I hung up as when we started talking.)

Then I got a call from Operations that Hughes was looking at property near Rancho Santa Fe (near San Diego). He wanted me to be ready to move there on a moment's notice. Since it all seemed tentative, I simply said that I'd wait for their next call, although I think they took that as a signal that I was ready to go. Virgie and I had a long talk, and we agreed that if I got that call I'd look the situation over. If it seemed to be a job with a future, I'd stay; if not, I'd pick up my option to take a hike. But that second call never came.

About six months later Kay Glenn called me. He wanted me to come by Operations for a chat. When I got there he seemed to be in a good mood. I was trying to figure out why he was doing his old-buddy routine when he lowered the boom.

"Ron, you've been told to stay at home and wait to hear from Mr. Hughes. We feel that you haven't been following those instructions." Before I could open my mouth to frame an alibi, he continued, "You've been working for the Burkett Fence Company in Culver City for the past several months." He went on to tell me who I had called on over the past weeks, what prices I had quoted, whether I had gotten the job, and more information that I would have thought was hard to come by. I began to curse myself for not paying attention to my rear-view mirror, but that is one of the luxuries of being a free man. Then I realized—I *was* free. A decision I hadn't been prepared to make had been made for me, and it felt good. I was free of Hughes and his organization. They were finally, after 14 months, going to let me quit. I began to laugh, and I laughed so long and so loud that Glenn probably thought I was nuts.

While I was off the payroll, that wasn't to be my last connection with Hughes Productions. I would often have lunch, and one for the road after work, at a restaurant on La Cienega Boulevard. I had met one of the regulars and knew that he had a responsible job at Hughes Aircraft. He knew that I had once been very closely associated with Hughes, but he didn't know what I had done.

At that time Hughes was under fire from the management of TWA, which was claiming that his handling of the financing for the jet fleet had damaged the airline.

Lawsuits were being filed right and left, and there was a small army of subpoena bearers in L.A., looking for Hughes.

One evening I stopped for a homeward-bound drink and the guy from Hughes Aircraft came up to me. That in itself was unusual, since we generally went no further than a nod and a hello. Then he bought me a drink. I sat there trying to figure out what could be next, and sure enough, he made his pitch.

"Ron, I've got some friends in town who have a big job to do. They have asked for my help. I know that you were an insider with Howard Hughes and that you still have good connections within the organization." I decided not to open my mouth. "They need someone to lay a piece of paper on him, and are prepared to pay hand-somely for it." He sat back and waited for my answer.

"Write that handsome figure on the back of this nap-kin," I said. (It seemed the mysterious thing to do.)

He took the napkin, wrote something, folded it, and handed it back to me. I unfolded it and read the number: $25,000. I began to laugh.

"If you're serious about this," I said, "you'd better add a zero to what you've written there. Oh, and one other thing. That amount is to be deposited in escrow at my bank before I ever make an effort to serve that paper." He looked as if I'd gone nuts. "Tell your people that I read the papers, too. I know that they're looking to get a $100 *million* judgment if they win, and they think they *will* win if they can force Hughes on the stand. So it seems to me that $250,000 is awfully cheap to pay to the guy who can do what they need done." He said that he'd get back to his people, and then get back to me. (He never came back with any word. In fact, he never spoke to me again.)

But I thought about that meeting for a couple of days, and the more I thought the more pissed off I got. I couldn't believe that such a highly placed employee was trying to burn the Old Man. I decided I'd try and frustrate his efforts, so I called Kay Glenn.

"Kay, I had an interesting meeting with an employee of Hughes Aircraft, and I think you should know about it." I went on to tell him about the overture, and though I didn't identify the guy by name, Glenn seemed uninterested.

"Why would *anyone* bother to talk to you about something that concerns Mr. Hughes. *You* don't even work for him, and you don't even know where he is." I saw red. What the hell! I was going out of my way to tell him about a potential danger and he couldn't even bother to say thanks. In fact, he had to spit at me.

"Listen, you double bleep," I said, "I not only know where Howard Hughes *is,* I know how to get into the place." It was true. My fence selling took me into the most exclusive areas of L.A., and while I was going through Bel-Air I had seen enough familiar faces, cars, and operational procedures to verify the house that Hughes had to be in. I had then checked out the security and found that it was typical of most Hughes set-ups— lousy.

There was a 24-hour guard detail posted in the driveway, parked behind the gate that sealed off the driveway. But there was a road that went behind the property, and that road was unguarded. It was a simple matter to climb up a small embankment from the road to the pool level of the house. I knew it was simple because the first time I had gone back there I'd done it. When I got to the house I walked up to some sliding doors on the patio and looked inside. I didn't see Hughes, but then I didn't see a guard, either. I went up there to see if someone was on duty who I knew, but I didn't see anyone except the guy in the driveway, and he was a stranger.

Knowing all this, I said to Glenn, "If you give me your word that you won't make any phone calls to alert your guards at the house, I'll bet you a steak dinner that I can call you from the living room within the next hour."

Kay Glenn was *not* a betting man. "Why do you think that Mr. Hughes is in this area?" he wanted to know. I told him about seeing familiar faces in Bel-Air, and when I mentioned that the place I'd go to was 10001 Bel-Air Road, he got very quiet.

I got no thanks from him, and I don't know what happened to the guy at Hughes Aircraft. It's a matter of record that Hughes was never served a subpoena in the big TWA lawsuit, and though he lost it in the lower courts, he won on the final appeal to the Supreme Court. (Ironically, by the time the case had dragged its way up to the Supreme Court, Hughes had sold his interests in TWA for almost $550 million.) As of this writing, the case is now in the state courts in Delaware. It may wind up being the longest piece of litigation in the history of the American judicial system.

When I turned down the opportunity (such as it was) to serve Hughes with a subpoena and felt compelled to report the matter to Operations, I did so with no misgivings. Afterwards, though, I spent a lot of time trying to figure out why. I felt that I owed the organization nothing. I had worked for every cent I had been paid, including that 14-month period after I had quit. (I felt I'd earned that money not only to make up for what had happened in the past, but also because they expected me not to advance my career elsewhere and simply sit around at $125 a week.) My health had suffered, and I had been kicked off the payroll against the express promise of Howard Hughes. (I still think that Hughes himself figures that I'm on the payroll, at a living wage, and am waiting for his call.)

It finally seemed that I did what I did out of sheer loyalty to Howard Hughes. Yeah, I still liked the old rascal. We'd had our differences, our arguments. He'd told me some white lies and I'd told him some. But, on balance, he had never really treated me with anything less than respect. He gave me credit for my intelligence, humor, dedication to an impossible job, and loyalty. He had, under his own pressures (and I'd *bet* that pinworms was one of them), pushed me hard, but he'd had the good sense and decency to back off when he knew that he had gone too far. Yes, that was it: I found myself admitting that I liked Howard Hughes.

And you know, I still do.